Ten Lies My Family Told Me

Jewish Family History Secrets Revealed

RICHARD BEACH

FOR KAREN

Who knows all my secrets,
but stays married to me anyway.

CONTENTS

FAMILY TREE

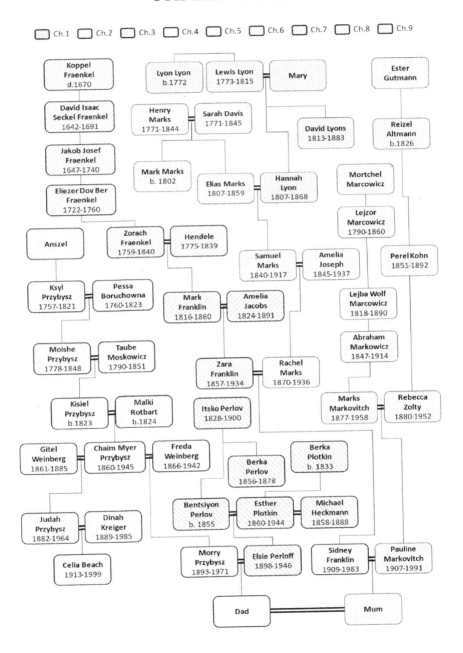

□ Ch.1 □ Ch.2 □ Ch.3 □ Ch.4 □ Ch.5 □ Ch.6 □ Ch.7 □ Ch.8 □ Ch.9

Koppel Fraenkel d.1670

David Isaac Seckel Fraenkel 1642-1691

Jakob Josef Fraenkel 1647-1740

Eliezer Dov Ber Fraenkel 1722-1760

Lyon Lyon b.1772

Lewis Lyon 1773-1815

Mary

Ester Gutmann

Henry Marks 1771-1844

Sarah Davis 1771-1845

David Lyons 1813-1883

Reizel Altmann b.1826

Mark Marks b. 1802

Elias Marks 1807-1859

Hannah Lyon 1807-1868

Mortchel Marcowicz

Lejzor Marcowicz 1790-1860

Anszel

Zorach Fraenkel 1759-1840

Hendele 1775-1839

Samuel Marks 1840-1917

Amelia Joseph 1845-1937

Perel Kohn 1851-1892

Ksyl Przybysz 1757-1821

Pessa Boruchowna 1760-1823

Mark Franklin 1816-1860

Amelia Jacobs 1824-1891

Lejba Wolf Marcowicz 1818-1890

Moishe Przybysz 1778-1848

Taube Moskowicz 1790-1851

Zara Franklin 1857-1934

Rachel Marks 1870-1936

Abraham Markowicz 1847-1914

Kisiel Przybysz b.1823

Malki Rotbart b.1824

Itsko Perlov 1828-1900

Marks Markovitch 1877-1958

Rebecca Zolty 1880-1952

Gitel Weinberg 1861-1885

Chaim Myer Przybysz 1860-1945

Freda Weinberg 1866-1942

Berka Perlov 1856-1878

Berka Plotkin b. 1833

Judah Przybysz 1882-1964

Dinah Kreiger 1889-1985

Bentsiyon Perlov b. 1855

Esther Plotkin 1860-1944

Michael Heckmann 1858-1888

Celia Beach 1913-1999

Morry Przybysz 1893-1971

Elsie Perloff 1898-1946

Sidney Franklin 1909-1983

Pauline Markovitch 1907-1991

Dad

Mum

i

MAP OF EUROPE
(Borders are shown as of approx. 1880-1890)

FOREWORD

Like most Anglo-Jewish families, when I asked my parents about 'where we came from' (meaning family history, not the birds and bees – that would be a *very* different book), the answer was sketchy and dismissive. We are a family of Ashkenazi Jews, so of course it all started in a tiny, impossible to pronounce village just outside Warsaw, from which we came penniless to England and bravely pulled ourselves up by our bootstraps using nothing but hard work, quick wit, and strong family bonds. Those that didn't move to England or America were lost in the Shoah – no names, no records, all gone. And as for tracing this backwards? Don't even bother. The Poles, Germans and Russians wouldn't waste their time looking after any records of Jewish lives, even if such records still existed. Don't look back, look forward. We're Her Majesty's Loyal Jews now, and part of the UK immigrant success story to which more recently arrived communities can only aspire.

I've now been researching my own family history, on and off, for over thirty years. And while a lot of what my parents and wider family told me has indeed proved to be true, almost all of what I've said in the previous paragraph has turned out to be not quite the case. My family history is a lot more complex than I was told. It's a story than includes crime, wealth, war, politics, revolution, tragedy, royalty, deception, scandal, and a great deal more. So rather than writing a chronological history or a collection of mini-biographies from the information I have unearthed, I've chosen ten things which turned out to be not exactly the way I was led to expect. In doing so, I hope that I can shine a little more light on the experiences of my own family, and how that might inform the way we see migrants and minorities today.

1 We'll Never Know Grandpa's Birthday

The first book I ever wrote was about family history. It was a project in Class 2 of my primary school, when I would have been just turning ten in the late 1970s (the class numbers counted backwards, so you turned eleven in Class 1, then left to go on to secondary school). We were given the task of writing a biography of any person we chose. My decision on the subject of my book was an easy one – my maternal grandfather, whom I knew as my 'Poppa'. I was already transfixed on a regular basis by his stories of growing up in the East End of London, and of his wartime experiences as part of Montgomery's 8th Army across Egypt, North Africa, Italy, Holland and Germany. Our books – a massive 20 pages long – were planned, drafted, carefully handwritten (in pencil) and then illustrated before being bound like a 'proper' book between cardboard covers.

I still have the book; it's one of my most treasured possessions, along with my Poppa's medals and the photographs I have of him in uniform. Although he was sometimes given to exaggeration in the interests of entertaining his grandsons, the contents of the book are pretty accurate. I found out a great deal about my Poppa's life and I'm so glad that I still have it. Nevertheless, there's one sentence in my book which, in its brevity, speaks volumes about how differently the two sides of my family history were presented to me even at that early age. I included the fact that Poppa's daughter – my mum – got married in September 1960. In mentioning my dad, I added one short sentence to cover everything I knew about his family history: "*His father was Polish, and had lost all his passport papers.*"

And that was all that I had been told about my other grandfather – the one who wasn't Poppa, but Grandpa. He died when I was only two years old, so I have no memory of him besides the kind of half-real memory that comes from looking at old photos or films that you are in, leading you to believe that you do remember because you must have been there. My dad's dad – whom I knew as Morry Beach, although his original surname was 'something unpronounceable with no vowels' – was from Poland, but that was all I knew. I can't recall exactly what my dad would tell me whenever I asked about where the Beaches came from, but by the age of ten I clearly had a picture in my head of a refugee in such a hurry to get to England that he had no documentation and probably no luggage either. The one other thing that we were always told about Grandpa was easy to remember, as we were reminded of it at the same time every year. On the Jewish festival of Purim (which falls on a different secular date each year), Dad would raise a glass and wish his own father a happy birthday – because, he always told me, Grandpa arrived in England without even knowing what day he was born. So the family adopted Purim as the day on which they would celebrate his birthday.

It didn't occur to ten-year-old me to ask a few more questions about this. How old was Grandpa when he came to England, not to know the date of his own birthday? And if he was that young, what about his parents – wouldn't they have known? Or his brothers and sisters? (I vaguely knew that Dad had some cousins with the same surname as us). But no, I never questioned it – and throughout my childhood, the family story was quite clear; Grandpa's actual birthday was lost. If it had been recorded at the time back in Poland, there was no way that those records would have survived the chaos of two world wars. My father also made it clear that he had no idea what year his father was actually born – there was an age on his gravestone, but Dad would always tell me that he was sure that was wrong.

I was in the Sixth Form – around seventeen years old – when I started to get this nagging feeling that I wanted to know more about my family history. I'm not sure where that came from, but I remember talking about it incessantly with my classmates, who were of course not so enthusiastic to listen. I told them that my surname shouldn't really be Beach, but instead some unpronounceable Eastern European name that I'll never find out. Their response was to nickname me "Beachowski" and otherwise tell me to shut up, which I think was probably reasonable enough.

At university, family history became relevant again when I was instructed – as a Geography student – to come up with a topic for my third year dissertation. The dissertation never actually got completed (I changed subjects for my third year), but I had written an outline of the idea I wanted to investigate. It centred around migration; I wanted to use my family history to see if it was true that once an immigrant family started moving out from their initial location in the centre of a new city, they would continue to move steadily outwards along the same arterial routes. This took me back to my Grandpa Morry, who arrived from Poland (as far as I knew) into the West End of London before moving out to Kilburn and Cricklewood; then my parents moved to Kenton, and then further out to Pinner – following the tracks of the Metropolitan Line out of London and deeper into the leafy suburbs. I saw myself eventually living somewhere even further out – Chorleywood or Amersham. Meanwhile, I knew even then that my Mum's side of the family had followed a very different route, starting in the East End and moving steadily northwards through Mile End, Bethnal Green and Hackney before picking up the line of the Old North Road (now more familiar as the A10) to Tottenham and Palmers Green. In marrying my dad, Mum had jumped westwards – opting out of a sequence that would have carried her further out along the A10 towards Enfield and Waltham Abbey.

The little bits of research I did into my family's geographical spread outwards from Central London gave me a taste for seeing how far back I could go – was there anything more to be found? So I undertook the usual first task for any budding genealogist; finding some old relatives, and asking them what they could tell me about the family. There was one relative on Dad's side who, he assured me, would be my best bet for this kind of information – Auntie Celia. Very possibly the first Beach to be born in the UK, and certainly the first person in the family to be born with our current surname.

Celia was Dad's half-cousin, and with her help I was able to start piecing together the Beach family tree. It centred around my great-grandfather Myer (for whom I'm named, as my Hebrew name which is used to identify me in any religious context is *Meir*), who married two sisters. With the older sister he fathered a boy, Celia's father Uncle Joe (more about him – a lot more – in Chapter 8). Then the older sister died, and Myer married the younger sister with whom he fathered the rest of my Dad's uncles and aunts, plus of course my Grandpa. So Celia's dad (Joe) and my Grandpa were half-brothers, but at the same time their DNA inheritance was as alike as full brothers. This was just the beginning of the family tree getting complicated.

I spent a great afternoon with Celia in her Hampstead townhouse, drinking tea and being told story after story. In my inexperience as a researcher, I failed to record the interview and all I came away with were just a few scribbles on the back of an envelope. But what I had was invaluable; the "little village just outside Warsaw" had a name, and so did my family. We were, before we came to London, the family Przybysz. Joe, the first of the family to arrive here, got frustrated with customers finding it so difficult to write cheques out to a name whose only value seemed to be as a Scrabble score. So he took the second half of his name – "bysz" – and Anglicised it to Beach. Then he brought his brothers and sisters, and his parents, over from Poland in the years leading up to the First World War.

Celia also confirmed the name of their Polish *shtetl* (village). It was Rawa Mazowiecka, about half-way between Warsaw and the industrial town of Łodz in the centre of Poland. So this was where Grandpa was born. Dad and I went to Bushey cemetery to confirm Grandpa's age at death (Dad was still sure that it was wrong, but it gave me something to go on), and his father's name (from the Hebrew inscription on a Jewish gravestone, which always includes a patronymic). Grandpa Morry's gravestone confirmed his Hebrew name as *Moshe ben Meir* (Moses, son of Myer) and suggested that he was born in 1897 or early 1898.

A visit to Rainham Cemetery in East London enabled me to find the grave of Myer, and that of his second wife – the younger of the two sisters, born Freda Weinberg. This gave me their dates and patronymics too; Freda died first in 1942 aged 78, meaning that she was born in 1864. Her Hebrew name reads *Fradel Bat Yeshiya*, which translates to Freda daughter of – Isaiah? I wasn't sure and that was my best guess (I have since confirmed that this name is *Szaia* in Polish, or *Shaya* in Yiddish). As for Myer, he was (according to his gravestone) at the grand old age of 97 when he died in 1945, suggesting a birth year of 1848. His Hebrew name appears as *Meyer ben Katriel*. Katriel? I'd not come across that name before at all, and given the state of the lettering on his gravestone I wasn't even sure if I had identified the characters correctly.

So that was as much as I knew so far. Grandpa was born Morry Przybysz in 1897 or 1898 in Rawa Mazowiecka to Myer and Freda. Myer Przybysz was born in 1848, presumably also in Rawa. As for his father, all I had was a possible name – Katriel – about which I really wasn't sure. And it looked like that was all I was ever going to know.

By now it was the summer of 1990. Having graduated from university, I was spending the summer travelling as part of an inter-varsity initiative between UK and US universities – a trip which took myself and three American students around Europe to run debating workshops in English for European students. The main part of the trip (and I'm convinced to this day it was some kind of CIA operation) took place in Eastern Europe, where formerly Communist educational institutions were starting to wake up after the fall of the Iron Curtain, hungry for a sweet taste of Western Democracy and all the parliamentary tricks that come with it. I got to see the Baltic States just before they became independent from the USSR, and Moscow just as power was slipping from Gorbachev's Soviet Union to Yelstin's Russia. But before that, I spent a week in Poland. I flew into Warsaw, and was staying in the university at Łodz (which, I now learned, is pronounced "Woodjh"). It was an opportunity I simply couldn't pass up.

Looking at the map, I could see that it would only require a small diversion to take the E67 rather than the direct E30 from Warsaw to Łodz, and then we could pass through my grandpa's birthplace – Rawa Mazowiecka. As our flight was a little late and we were running behind schedule, I was only allowed enough time to get out of the car, breathe the air of the town where my ancestors lived, have a look around and grab a quick photo before resuming our bumpy journey to Łodz.

To be honest, I could see exactly why my family would have been eager to leave Rawa Mazowiecka. I'm sure I wasn't seeing it at its best, but it wasn't pretty. The attitude of our Polish host didn't do too much to help; the next day, as we walked around Łodz, he apologised for the ugliness of the older buildings on the basis that they were built at a time when, as he said with a disapproving sneer, "the Jews owned everything". More reminders that Joe was right to leave, and to bring the rest of the family over.

I can't remember how I found out about the Mormons. It must have been from a library book on genealogy, which led me to visit the Hyde Park Chapel of the Church of Jesus Christ of Latter Day Saints, on Exhibition Road in South Kensington opposite London's Science and Natural History Museums. By the time this happened, I was a geography teacher whose duties included occasionally taking classes to visit the geological galleries of the Natural History Museum. On one such visit with a sixth form class, the students were happy to find their own way home and I was left with the perfect opportunity to visit the Chapel and see how the Mormons could help me learn more about my family. Perhaps I should explain here, for those who might be unaware, what the connection is between genealogy and the Church of Jesus Christ of Latter Day Saints. The Mormon faith includes the belief that even after death, family members can be baptised and therefore saved from damnation. This has resulted in the Church collecting huge amounts of genealogical data from across the world in the form of over 2 million rolls of microfilms locked away behind 14-ton doors in the Granite Mountain Records Vault in Salt Lake City – copies of which could be ordered and viewed in Mormon Family History Centres around the world, including the one downstairs from the Hyde Park Chapel.

And it wasn't long before I had reason to believe, contrary to what I had previously been told, that I could order microfilms of the 19th century birth, marriage and death records of the Jewish community of Rawa Mazowiecka. I looked up the details of what had been photographed onto microfilm, and found my first setback - the years for which I could view records ranged between 1824 and 1866, with some gaps within that range. So any record of Grandpa's birth (sometime in the late 1890s, I guessed) wouldn't be there. But Myer was – according to his gravestone – born in 1848! I should be able to confirm his father's name and maybe find out much more about the Przybysz family history. I ordered the relevant microfilms and waited the two weeks until they had been sent over from Salt Lake City.

The second setback was my inability to read the records – the Mormons had photographed whatever was in the archives in Poland, and the microfilms contained image after image of dense handwritten nineteenth century Polish text. I could barely read the words, let alone translate them. Fortunately, the Hyde Park Family History Centre had a guide to these records, enabling me to make some sense of them. Some years had an index of surnames at the end of the year's records, but for other years it was a case of looking through every single birth, marriage and death record to check for the elusive Przybysz surname. Fortunately, one good thing about being a teacher doing family history research is the time you get in the school holidays. With the benefit of days to spend sitting at the microfilm readers painstakingly trawling through records, I was able to find all the Przybysz records in the Rawa files.

The third setback – Myer wasn't there. Not every year had been preserved, but I had the birth records for 1848 and there was no sign of him. The nearest I could find was the birth of a boy named *Mosiek*

Hersz Przybysz in 1849. As for the Hebrew name of Mosiek Hersz's father (his signature in Hebrew letters appears at the bottom of the record), it looked to me to be something like *Yekusiel*, which wasn't a Hebrew name I knew – and didn't sound like Katriel either. I found a few more Przybyszs, but nothing that linked to what I knew about the Przybysz family members who moved to London.

Then the Internet happened. Suddenly, the World Wide Web was somewhere that could give everyone access to huge amounts of information as various organisations put records, lists, databases and transcripts online. And being digital, it was the work of milliseconds to do what had previously taken hours when searching for a specific surname or location.

By the late noughties, JRI-Poland (https://jri-poland.org/) had amassed hundreds of thousands of indexed and searchable records, from more than a thousand locations across Poland. Even better than that, they had indexed sets of records held in the Polish archives at Grodzisk Mazowiecki (which included records from nearby Rawa Mazowiecka) covering the period from the 1870s to around 1898; could Grandpa's elusive birth record be there?

These records had been indexed, but not digitised – so on the JRI-Poland site, I could see the year, the name, the record number and whether it was a birth, marriage or death. If I wanted to know any more, I would need to contact the archives themselves in Grodzisk, and pay for them to scan the records I was interested in and send them over to me. This proved more difficult than it might now seem – although it was the year 2010, I had to send a letter (in Google Translate Polish and in English, to be on the safe side) requesting the 7 or 8 records that looked worth investigating, and then wait for a response which would tell me how much the service would cost, and how to organise an international bank transfer to clear the funds.

Nevertheless, the indexes that were available on the JRI-Poland website gave me a lot to hope for – there were a string of Przybysz births in the decade from 1883 to 1893, ending with two Przybysz births; records 59 and 60 in 1893 – a girl named Ruchla, and a boy named Moszek Mordka. Grandpa Morry did have a sister called Rushka (like Ruchla, a familiar version of Rachel) – did she have a twin? (Dad didn't seem to think so). Then it struck me: Grandpa Morry's Hebrew name was Moshe (Moses), which in Poland would be Moszek – and could Morry be a familiar version of Mordechai, which in Poland would be Mordka? Were Grandpa and Aunt Rushka twins? (Again, Dad didn't seem to think so; in fact this theory made no sense at all to him).

I was at work when the email arrived – from the Grodzisk archives, telling me quite simply, if Google Translate was to be trusted, that the funds had been cleared and the hardcopies of the scanned records were on their way. What I wasn't expecting was that the scanned images were also attached to the email – the answers were right here! Nervously, I opened the attachments to see if I could decipher the answers that had eluded me for so long.

I immediately realised that it would take some time to do any such deciphering. These records were different from the ones I had made sense of years ago from the Mormon microfilms. After the 1863 January Uprising demanding Polish independence from the Russian Empire had been brutally crushed, every official document in Poland had to be in Russian. I was now looking at dense paragraphs of nineteenth century handwriting in the Russian language and, most importantly, in the Cyrillic alphabet. Working out what these records could tell me was going to take a lot longer than I thought. Grandpa's birthday remained a mystery.

But thanks to the prolific power of the internet and many an evening spent ignoring my wife and children (that's their version of events, at least) with my nose buried in Russian-English dictionaries, I was able to work out what I had in front of me. Moszek Mordka <u>was</u> Grandpa Morry. His parents were named as Chaim Myer Przybysz (which in Cyrillic is *Хаумъ Маеръ Прзубъуцъ*, to give you an idea of how easy this was to decipher) and Freda Weinberg - perfect matches for the great-grandparents of mine buried in Rainham Cemetery. And as for Ruchla/Rushka, she wasn't his twin – although her birth had been registered in 1893 alongside Morry's, she had actually been born three years earlier in 1890. I can only imagine that Myer hadn't thought it worth the trip to the Town Hall to register the birth of a girl, and just waited until the next time he had to register a son. I'd like to think that this was because he was incredibly busy in his work as a kosher butcher, diligently meeting the needs of the community. Of course, that may not have been the case at all; it could have been simple nineteenth century sexism, or even just laziness (a trait which I can certainly say I have to have inherited from *somewhere*). Finally, I was in a position to learn the one snippet of information that I had always imagined to be forever lost – the actual date of Grandpa's birthday! Except…there were two dates on the birth record. It says quite clearly that Grandpa was born on the twenty fifth of April. And, equally clearly, that he was born on the seventh of May.

This was a situation which I had anticipated; by this point in my genealogical investigations, I was no longer so naïve as to assume that any of it would be straightforward. There are two dates on Morry's birth record for the same reason that the 1917 Russian Revolution – known as the October Revolution – actually happened in November. And for the same reason that Christmas for the Russian Orthodox Church falls in early January. As part of the "Russification" of Poland, official documents had two dates; the first according to the Julian calendar (used in Russia), and the second – 12 days 'later' in the calendar – according to the Gregorian calendar used in Poland and the rest of Europe.

I had no difficulty in deciding which one was the right date to choose. I took a deep breath, called Dad and told him that if he wanted to raise a glass on Morry's birthday, he should do so each year on the seventh of May. Or, if he wanted to use the Jewish calendar, the twenty-first day of the Hebrew month of Iyyar – more than two months after the festival of Purim.

Which leaves only one mystery: if he was born in 1893, he would have been about twenty years old when he came to London. Why would he deliberately tell his children that he didn't know when his birthday was? I don't think any document sitting an archive somewhere can answer that one for me. That, we might never know.

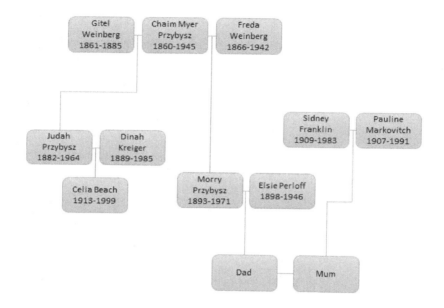

My first book – a biography of my grandfather Sidney Franklin, written a few years before his death

Me with Grandpa Morry

The first Beach back in Rawa for decades, July 1990

*The Beach family in 1925 — my great-grandparents Freda and Myer are in
the centre, seated; Grandpa Morry is in the back row, third from the left*

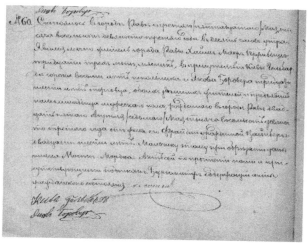

*Grandpa Morry's birth record, giving us his actual birthday at last (image
courtesy of the Polish State Archives in Warsaw, Grodzisk Mazowiecki
branch)*

2 The Respectable Branch of the Family

In family legend, the Marks branch of the family are the respectable ones. That was only ever in relative terms of course (no pun intended); it wasn't that they were so impressive, but every other branch of the family – I was told – was either from the very bottom of the East End social heap, or else virtually still wiping the mud of Eastern Europe off our shoes. The Marks family, on the other hand, had been in England for two centuries; they had lived in the West End; there was even a whispered hint that the surname had originally been *Marquez*, and we had noble Sephardi blood in our veins. If there was anything to be proud of, the Marks lineage was the place to look.

Marks was the maiden surname of my mum's dad's mum – my great-grandmother Rachel Marks, who married Zara Franklin in 1906 and subsequently gave birth to three boys and a girl. The middle one of those three boys was my Poppa (and war hero, according to him at least) Sidney Franklin. Once married to Zara, Rachel settled with him in Mile End and stayed for the rest of her life in the heart of Jewish East London – and beyond really, as she is buried in East Ham Jewish cemetery. But I was told that there were connections here in much more upmarket parts of London – Rachel had some rich relations, and if nothing else the records I would be searching through would be in a language and an alphabet that I could understand.

I've managed to trace the Marks line back into the eighteenth century, but not beyond the shores of England. Which is quite something really – in 1771, when the earliest Marks ancestor of whom I can be sure was born, the Jewish population of England was a mere ten thousand. Most of these were in London or in port towns where they would have arrived from Europe and continued to trade with Holland and Germany. This first Marks was the very English-sounding and respectable Henry Marks (Hebrew name Zvi Hertz). Unlike other branches of the family, Henry appears in a document which isn't simply a record of a birth, marriage or death, but evidence of his property; an insurance policy dated 15th June 1802, describing "Henry Markes" as a Gold and Silver Refiner. Okay, the address wasn't in the West End, it was Sandy's Row off Petticoat Lane – but that was where most of the community lived at that time, and he was virtually in the City of London itself. His house was insured for £100, his stock (of precious metals, presumably) at a further £50, and then his own possessions at another £50 – this was clearly someone who had some substance to look after. A note on the policy shows that it was still being renewed eleven years later.

Two hundred pounds was a lot of money in 1800, but when considered as the sum total of one's possessions it works out as the equivalent of about £17,000 today; not exactly wealthy, but significant enough to need insuring. Henry was, as far as I could see, a solid entrepreneur working on his own account and prosperous enough to insure his house and workplace at a time when many of the poorer classes would not have done so. And at least he was involved with gold, even if he didn't get to keep much of it. A London Directory of Professions and Trades from 1811 lists Henry as a refiner and dealer in gold & silver, so this was clearly someone with some stability and economic longevity. This was looking like the source of what wealth there may have been in the family.

There was one other record that Henry left behind from even earlier in his career. On 17th February 1796, while still in his early twenties, Henry was involved in a trial at London's Central Criminal Court (the "Old Bailey") which possibly related to his metalworking career. The charge was providing counterfeit coin. Unfortunately, Henry was in the dock, accused of trying to sell five counterfeit coins to a certain Levi Cowen. Coining offences were technically treason at that time, coming under the category of Offences Against The King; sentences given for such offences through the 1790s ranged from imprisonment for 12 months, through transportation, to – in a number of cases – the death penalty.

Levi Cowen told the Court his story. In his version of events, Henry had approached him on a Sunday morning and offered to sell him counterfeit coins. Cowen didn't have the real money on him to pay, so he said he would come back to Henry's house later. He did so, but this time with an officer and another witness – and lo and behold, the counterfeit money was found – along with a frying-pan on the stove with molten metal in it, which Cowen clearly saw as evidence of Henry's counterfeiting work. But on cross-examination, it became clear that Cowen had given a slightly different account when previously questioned – and that the officer in question didn't entirely trust him in the first place. When asked *"What are you?"*, the court transcript tells us that Cowen answered, *"A Jew, and I sell lemons and oranges."*

Once Cowen had finished at the witness stand, the others who accompanied him to Henry's house gave their testimony. Things at this point start to look a little better for Henry, as the officer and the other witness make it fairly clear that they couldn't be sure that Cowen didn't have the counterfeit coins with him all along. Finally we hear from Henry himself, my great-great-great-great-grandfather. With a strangely heroic and noble simplicity, his contribution is only twenty-four words: *"I am now, in this present situation, an innocent man; I never saw the evidence before in my life till he came up stairs."*

Then, the twist that no courtroom drama should be without. Only a single witness for the defence is recorded following Henry himself; a certain Moses Cowen. The next part of the transcript could be from a soap opera:

COUNSEL: *Do you know Levi Cowen?*

MOSES: *To my sorrow, he is my unfortunate son.*

COUNSEL: *What is his general character?*

MOSES: *If I must speak the truth, I must speak against my son.*

COUNSEL: *Is your son fit to be believed upon his oath?*

MOSES: *I would not take his oath for three halfpence; he has taken so many false oaths.*

That settled it. Four character witnesses appeared on Henry's behalf, and I cannot imagine that it took the jury long to return a verdict of Not Guilty. Young Henry Marks walked free with no stain on his character. (As for Levi Cowen, I was hoping to find evidence that he came to a sticky end before too long, but no such records seem to exist – perhaps his father's harsh words set his moral compass straight? Maybe that's a nicer thought. Yes, let's say that Levi became a reformed character and a pillar of the community.)

By 1836, in his mid-sixties with Cowen's attempt at framing him just a distant memory, Henry can be found in Paget's A-Z Commercial London Directory as "Henry Marks & Son Gold and Silver Refiners". At least two of his sons joined him in the refining trade – Mark his eldest son born in 1802 just as Henry was taking out his insurance, and his second son Elias (my great-great-great-grandfather). The respectable Marks dynasty was taking shape.

There are two Yiddish words – both based on Hebrew equivalents – which perhaps represent the two extremes of what impact your children can have on you, particularly in your later years. *Naches* (from the Hebrew *Nachat*) literally means "comfort", but can also mean pride, joy and a range of other positive emotions which can swell within one's heart and give one a warm glow of satisfaction that all will be well with one's offspring. In contrast, *Tsuris* (from the Hebrew *Tzarot*) means "troubles" or woe, with all the corresponding despair and depression that ensue as one worry piles upon another. King David himself, the very model of Jewish achievement and kingship, went to his grave filled with *tsuris* from his children – his firstborn Amnon had raped his own half-sister Tamar, his favourite son Absalom had been killed trying to usurp the throne, while his surviving sons Adonijah and Solomon were squabbling over the succession.

By the time Henry died on 14th February 1844, his *nachas* had almost certainly turned to *tsuris* thanks to his sons Mark and Elias. The younger of the two brothers was at least there to be with him as he died of "Gout and Old Age" at 8 Sandy's Row, the same house which he had insured more than four decades before – Elias was named as the informant on Henry's death certificate, present at his father's passing. Mark, on the other hand, was just about as far away as he could possibly be from his father and brother.

As Henry breathed his last, his firstborn son was spending his tenth day ashore in Van Diemen's Land – modern-day Tasmania – having spent four months at sea on *HMS Anson* alongside 498 other male convicts sentenced to be transported to the other side of the world, so that Britain could be rid of such criminal undesirables. His crime? Receiving stolen goods, namely nine gold rings belonging to William Thomas Middleton.

The exact timeline of the events that led to Mark being sent to Van Diemen's Land can be pieced together from newspaper reports and court records, although these do not always agree on all the details. What they appear to agree on is that on 3rd May 1843, Middleton – a jeweller and watchmaker in Commercial Road, East London – was the victim of a smash-and-grab robbery, with upwards of £150 of jewellery taken. The next day, Mark was seen buying a number of gold rings at a knock-down price. Two further witnesses said that later that same day they bought rings from Mark, also at prices much lower than one would normally expect to pay.

Only a week after the robbery, some of the stolen goods had been identified and traced back to Mark. He was arrested and detained at the King of Prussia public house on 10th May, but protested his innocence. On 18th May he was locked up at the police station, and came up for trial at the Old Bailey on 12th June. The authorities must have thought that they had the thief, as the charge was robbery – like his father nearly 50 years before, the death penalty was not unthinkable as a possible outcome. Fortunately, some kind of justice prevailed as there was, the judge agreed, insufficient evidence that Mark was involved in the robbery itself. On the judge's advice, the jury found him not guilty.

Mark walked free — but was arrested the next day on the charge of knowingly receiving stolen goods. He was tried twice for this crime, relating to different items of the haul. His first trial for receiving, at the Middlesex Sessions rather than the Old Bailey, ended on 20th June with another not guilty verdict. But next time, the evidence was a lot more compelling. His third and final trial in connection with the Middleton robbery was on 3rd July 1843. Although one of the witnesses against Mark (a rival refiner called Reeves, who was probably just as guilty himself) was discredited to the point where the judge threatened to put him in the dock with Mark, the jury decided that Mark knew full well that the rings were stolen property. To be honest, I think they were probably right. My distant uncle may not have been a thief, but the circles in which he mixed were certainly populated with shady characters, and I don't doubt that he took occasional advantage of such events to help make a living. He was sentenced to be transported "beyond the seas" for ten years.

The *Morning Post* newspaper from 6th July 1843 has a detailed report on Mark's trial, beginning with a very curious description which bears quoting here in full: "*Mark Marks, aged 41, a gold and silver refiner, of the Hebrew persuasion, and said to be a person of considerable wealth…*" Considerable wealth? I wonder if perhaps the newspaper is perhaps playing into the prejudices of some of its readers who might have been all too ready to believe in the greedy Jew, already rich but still unable to stop himself from acquiring more wealth from honest Englishmen through underhand means. As an odd postscript to the trial, on 22nd July the *Morning Post* reported on the trial of Solomon Hyams for the Middleton robbery. Again, the key witness for the prosecution was Reeves — and again, Reeves was reprimanded by the Court for his unreliable testimony (had it been a more enlightened legal system, I can't help wondering if Mark had good grounds for having his own sentence overturned after this).

Perhaps Mark's eventual conviction at the age of 41 was the

inevitable end to a sequence of court appearances and legal involvements stretching back a great deal further than the Middleton robbery. At the age of only 22, he spent a little over two months in Marshalsea Debtor's Prison in Southwark for insolvency. A year later in 1826, he was a witness to attempted theft and subsequent window-breaking at the King of Prussia Public House on Petticoat Lane – the very same pub where he would be detained seventeen years later. In 1832 he appears again as a witness, this time to the fatal beating of elderly Jewish pawnbroker Elias Hart by a certain William Bryant. Twelve years before Mark was sent across the world for receiving a few rings, Bryant was imprisoned for a mere twelve months for bludgeoning a man to death. Bryant's only defence was a written statement claiming that "he had been attacked in Petticoat-lane by several Jews, who surrounded and robbed him". There was no evidence to support such a claim.

No photograph of Mark has survived, so we cannot see an image of him – but the paperwork from his time as a prisoner gives a detailed description of him, if only for the purposes of identifying him should he attempt any kind of escape. The authorities were very specific about his height – five feet, four and a quarter inches (my mum's side of the family have never been giants). The 42-year-old had an oval head and visage of a fresh complexion, with reddish hair and whiskers. His light brown eyes sat below dark brown eyebrows and a forehead of medium height. The description goes on to say that he had "cupping marks" on both sides of both arms; this suggests that Mark had been subject to the efforts of the *Anson*'s surgeon Andrew Millar. Cupping was a popular treatment in the 1800s, involving the application of heated glass cups to the skin to draw toxins to the surface. Mark is recorded to have had a single day on the ship's sick list, for dysentery; perhaps cupping was the surgeon's response to this illness.

On arrival at Van Diemen's Land, Mark appears to have been almost the model prisoner. His convict report was only updated twice with minor breaches of the rules, and on 29 May 1849 he was given a Ticket of Leave. A Ticket of Leave allowed convicts to work for themselves if they remained in a specified area, reported regularly & attended divine worship every Sunday. A year later, his name appears in the Cornwall Chronicle, published in Launceston in Tasmania, in a list of prisoners granted Conditional Pardons. A Conditional Pardon allowed convicts freedom of the colony, but they were not permitted to return to the UK. Finally, at the very end of 1851 he is recorded as being discharged to Hobart as a free man – but there, the trail runs cold. What happened to Mark after nearly eight years as a prisoner remains unknown.

Meanwhile, in 1851 Mark's brother Elias was at the very heart of the British Empire's metropolis, not at its very farthest edge. The census of that year records Elias in residence at 5 Shepherd Street – a short road linking Oxford Street to Hanover Square, in the heart of London's West End. Today, this road is Dering Street W1, a part-pedestrianised lane of bars, art galleries and clothes shops on some of the most expensive real estate in the city. He is listed as a General Dealer, with his wife Hannah and three daughters - Sarah aged 21, Catherine aged 13 and Matilda aged 6 – as well as a house servant and two visitors who were staying in the house on the night of the census.

But this was not Elias's whole family. Just over a mile away in Covent Garden, another six of the Marks children can be found. The Head of the Household at number 9 Russell Place is the 18-year-old Rachel Marks, living with her brothers Harry (20), David (15) and Samuel (11) and sisters Julia (7) and Maria (3), as well as widowed aunt Rachel Lee and a servant with the rather royal name of Jane Seymour. Rachel's occupation is given as "Lodging House Keeper". From the backstreets of Whitechapel, here was a family spread across two West End properties, looking rather more prosperous than most Anglo-Jewish families of the time.

Except that the West End of the mid-nineteenth century was not quite the West End that it is now. Searching for mentions of Shepherd Street in newspapers of that era, the Times of October 30th 1844 reports of a woman "of loose and desperate character" who was charged with wilfully breaking the windows of Thomas Westlake, a general dealer in Bond Street. Westlake's crime, in the eyes of the window-breaking woman, was that he had been instrumental in helping the parish authorities of St. James Westminster in closing down a number of brothels in the area. The woman's address to the Court is reported in full:

"I shan't leave this world happy without putting my mark upon that --------. So help me G--, I'll smash every window in his house, and I'll smash him too the first chance I get. It's a wonder the Jews in Shepherd Street don't go altogether and knock his brains out. You may send me to prison, but as soon as I come out I'll be on the ------ again!"

If only we could know what those missing words actually were. But why would the Jews of Shepherd Street – which would have to include Elias - want to attack Westlake for his anti-brothel stance? Unfortunately, the obvious answer turned out to be the correct one. On 26 June of that year, Elias was found guilty at the Westminster Sessions of Keeping a Disorderly House, which is a rather euphemistic way of describing – well, exactly what I thought it was describing. A week later Elias and his wife Hannah were sentenced, with each of them being fined one pound. There was clearly a considerable campaign to clean up the area, and Elias was made to promise that such activities would be stopped, and the perpetrators moved out. It doesn't look like this is what happened, as the following year, 5 Shepherd Street was described as *"a common brothel of the lowest grade"* in a story of a respectable local wife and mother who was taken there and almost raped by an 'acquaintance' who plied her with drink first. Elias was still in Shepherd Street in 1851, and in the light of the use to which the building was put, the fact that there were two young 'visitors' staying the night when the census was taken starts to make a little more sense. One wonders whether the families of Harry Thomas and Susan Newman would be happy to know that their overnight stay in a low grade brothel was recorded for posterity. Susan's occupation is given as dressmaker, which was often the answer given by sex workers when they wished to give a more delicate trade (seamstress was another common euphemism used at the time).

Elias's association with sex work continued for at least four more years. In October 1855 an affidavit was submitted to the Middlesex Quarter Sessions titled *"The Queen against Marks and others, for misdemeanor"*. Once again, the honest tradesmen of Bond Street were lodging complaints against The Jews of Shepherd Street for, as the indictment says, *"severally keeping a common Bawdy House in the parish of Saint George Hanover Square"*. The result of this was not surprising; on 22nd November, at the Westminster Sessions themselves, Elias was found guilty of an offence listed simply as *"Bawdy House"*. More surprisingly, he was discharged *"on his own Recognition, To appear for Judgement When called on"* – and no record can be found of a sentence or punishment.

Henry Mayhew's famous work *London Labour and the London Poor*, written during the 1840s and 1850s when Elias was getting in and out of trouble for his involvement in prostitution, tells us that there were two kinds of Bawdy House – fully dedicated brothels where working girls were lodged, clothed, fed and boarded (in more than one sense of the word!) over an extended stay of months or years, and 'hotels' which simply provided rooms where sex workers could take their clients for a night or indeed for a much shorter period of time. It seems that Elias's properties in Shepherd Street and Russell Place were of the latter kind, since the only permanent residents of these properties were Elias's own family. If Mayhew is to be believed, Elias certainly would not have been short of potential business; Mayhew's book suggests that London was home to upwards of 80,000 prostitutes at the time.

Elias's last newspaper appearance was, unusually, as an innocent victim rather than as a criminal. By 1858, Shepherd Street had been renamed Union Street, and the campaign to give the area a better moral character was well underway. The property next door to Elias was now occupied by a range of small businesses including a carpenter and cabinet maker. While Number 6 may have been of much higher repute, this did not save it from a fire which started on the night of 6th April 1858 in the dry wooden materials of the workshop and quickly spread to the living quarters of the house, with the honest inhabitants forced to flee with their children having not even got dressed. The *Morning Chronicle* of the next day further reports that *"the flames rushed through the side wall into the private residence belonging to Mr. Marks, No.5, in the same street"*. Thankfully no lives were lost, and the municipal fire services were able to have the blaze dealt with by the middle of the following morning,

The blaze could not have been good for Elias's lungs. Those lungs would be the cause of his demise a year later, from Consumption (which we would now call tuberculosis) on 18th April 1859. He was 52 years old. One final puzzle which he has left us is the Occupation entry on his death certificate – "Dealer in Jewellery". Had Elias finally gone straight in the final years of his life, or did the informant who registered his death (one Coleman Isaacs, of whom more in a later chapter) decide that the safest option to spare the deceased's blushes was to give the occupation that he would have started with at the very beginning of his working life as the son Henry Marks the gold and silver refiner?

Probably not, I would argue. Sorry, great-great-great-grandpa Elias. The 1861 census shows his widow Hannah Marks still living at 5 Union Street as a "Hotel Keeper", which almost certainly means that she was carrying on the same occupation as before. With her were five daughters and one son, the 20-year-old General Dealer Samuel. Samuel would later move out to live most of his life as a prosperous businessman in leafy Barnsbury, married to Amelia and with twelve children - including Rachel, my Poppa's mum. What remains unknown is whether any of Samuel's children knew that their father grew up in a brothel.

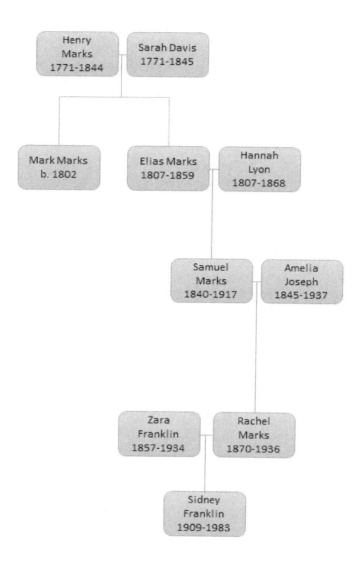

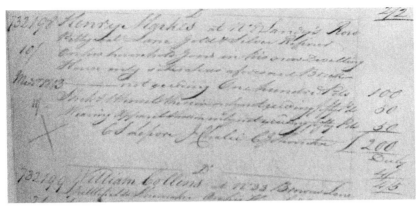

Henry Markes' insurance policy, 15ᵗʰ June 1802. Source: RSA Insurance Group Limited records held at the London Metropolitan Archives.

NEW COURT.

(Before the Common Serjeant.)

Mark Marks, aged 41, refiner, was indicted for feloniously receiving nine rings, &c., the property of William Thomas Middleton, well knowing the same to have been stolen.

The prisoner was tried at the last session of the Court for stealing the articles, which formed only part of a considerable amount of property stolen from the prosecutor, but from the total incompleteness of the evidence he was acquitted. He was then charged on the present indictment with receiving the property.

The jury returned a verdict of Guilty.

Sentence—Transportation for 10 years.

The London Evening Standard's report of Mark Marks' trial, 6ᵗʰ July 1843. Newspaper image © The British Library Board. All rights reserved. With thanks to The British Newspaper Archive (www.britishnewspaperarchive.co.uk)

Description of Mark Marks on his arrival in Van Diemen's Land, 1844.
Source: Tasmanian Archives CON18/1/41.

Conduct Record of Mark Marks, 1843-1851. Source: Tasmanian Archives
CON14/1/25, no. 11624.

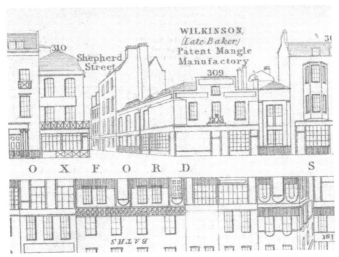

A profile view of Oxford Street in 1840. Elias & Hannah's hotel/brothel was part of the building below the words "Shepherd Street". (Source: David Rumsey Map Collection, David Rumsey Map Center, Stanford Libraries)

SUPPRESSION OF HOUSES OF ILL-FAME IN THE PARISH OF ST. GEORGE, HANOVER SQUARE.—A committee of the respectable inhabitants, of that notoriously infamous locality, Shepherd-street, Oxford street, was some time since formed, for the purpose of the suppression of various houses of ill-fame in that street, and finding all other means ineffectual, prosecutions were had, at the instance of the committee, against the keepers of the said houses. At the Westminster Sessions, the whole of the defendants pleaded guilty, and were held in sufficient bail to be called up for judgment, provided the nuisances complained of were not forthwith abated. We understand that the houses in question are being rapidly vacated by their respective occupiers, so that there is every probability that this long notorious street will at length be cleansed from its manifold impurities. We should suggest, in order to destroy as much as possible all associations with Shepherd-street, what has been done in similar cases, that the name be changed. A portion of the expenses incurred in the prosecutions will, by the 25th Geo. II., fall upon the parish.

Efforts to close down the brothels of Shepherd Street, as reported on 14th July 1844. Newspaper image © The British Library Board. All rights reserved. With thanks to The British Newspaper Archive (www.britishnewspaperarchive.co.uk)

3 The Poorest Chuts

Franklin is an English surname. Any search for the origin or meaning of this name will tell you that it derives from medieval times and the Middle English *frankelin*, meaning a "freeman" or a "landowner of free but not noble birth." Which is all very well, but I knew that it was extremely unlikely that my mum's family were tilling the soil of Merrie England in the 1300s, exchanging pleasantries with Dick Whittington or Geoffrey Chaucer (who wrote *The Franklin's Tale*). There were no Jews in England at that time between the expulsion in 1290 and readmission in the 1650s. So unless we're descended from a solid Anglo-Saxon yeoman who married into a Jewish family at some point, the surname must have some other derivation – or else it was just picked by a Jewish immigrant who wanted to sound English as they settled down in their adopted country.

As I started to trace my mum's paternal line backwards, everything I found appeared to confirm the suspicions that Mum held about the Franklin origins. My Poppa's dad – with the unusual given name of Zara – was indeed a lifelong inhabitant of the East End of London. He was born in 1857 in Palmer Street, in the heart of the "Tenter Ground" of Spitalfields. This area was named for the practice of hanging out cloths to dry on frames (called tenters), and it was an open space used by Flemish and Huguenot weavers who fled Catholic France in the 17th and 18th centuries to set up business in Protestant London. In 1829, as the weavers had moved on, the open space was developed into tenement housing with four short roads running between Tenter Street in the west and Shepherd Street in the East. It was in one of these humble tenement houses that Zara was born to Mark and Amelia Franklin.

Zara held down the same occupation for his entire working life as a Cigar Maker. While Mum had never (to her knowledge) been definitively told where the Franklins came from, she certainly had the impression that unlike most Ashkenazi Jewish families, it wasn't Poland or Russia. When pressed, the answer would keep coming back to her saying "well I think we might have been Dutch once upon a time." To which Dad would always respond (pronouncing the "ch" with a hard sound as in Loch Ness) "Aha! You're a *Chutee*!" much to my puzzlement. He did later explain that 'Chutees' was the way his family would always refer to the Dutch, although he didn't elaborate more than that.

Much later, I was pleasantly surprised to see that this all seemed to fit together. I now don't need to go further than Wikipedia to find that *"Chuts is the name applied to Jews who immigrated to London from the Netherlands.... they typically came from Amsterdam and practised trades they had already learned there, most notably cigar, cap and slipper making... they settled mostly in a small system of streets in Spitalfields known as the Tenterground."* It all fitted together neatly - the location, the occupation and even the timeline (Zara's parents Mark and Amelia were in Tilley Street, one of the streets built on the Tenter Ground, as early as 1851 just a year after they got married). I was confident that I would find Franklins in Holland among the large Ashkenazi community of Amsterdam or one of the outlying Dutch communities.

In the meantime, there was more to learn about the Franklins in Spitalfields. Zara's childhood could not have been an easy one – his father Mark died in November 1860 when Zara was only three years old. The circumstances of his passing make pretty grim reading; he died of meningitis in the Union Workhouse of Mile End, a week after having been admitted there for "Temporary Insanity." The descriptions of his occupation tell their own story; in 1851 he was a tailor, as he was again in 1857 on Zara's birth certificate. When admitted to the workhouse, he was described as a 'scourer' – still in the clothing industry, but a much less skilled job. At his death, his occupation is given simply as 'General Labourer'. It's difficult not to conclude that this was someone increasingly unable to ply his trade, suffering from physical and possibly mental illness too. Researching this branch of the family put me in touch with some long-lost distant cousins, who were able to provide a very grainy image of Mark. Despite a stiff collar, impressive whiskers and a bowler hat, he's not looking well at all.

Mark's death left his widow Amelia with five children aged from nine down to one. It is therefore hardly surprising that it was only a year and a half after Mark's death when she remarried. Her new husband – and probably the only father figure Zara would have remembered – was a Dutch cigar maker. Michael Nicklesberg was born in Amsterdam and arrived in London on the *Diana* in December 1855. He married Amelia in 1862, but six years later she was widowed again. Zara was only eleven. In the 1871 Census, Zara has his deceased stepfather's surname and occupation, and the alternative first name by which he was known for much of his life; he appears as the fourteen-year-old Charlie Nicklesberg, a cigar maker's assistant. Five years after that, he was lying about his age on his marriage certificate, claiming that he was 21 years old. (Neither 'Charlie' nor his new wife Esther signed the certificate but instead simply made their mark.)

Esther died in 1896, and Zara appears to have reverted to using both parts of his original name by the turn of the century. He remarried in 1906, and as he moved into his fifties he started a second family – which included my Poppa Sidney. From what I have been told, Zara seems to have been a complicated man; a gambler, a union organiser and an absent parent. I wonder if the poverty, instability and trauma of his early life led to a somewhat selfish approach to the way he behaved as an adult. I can confidently say that my Poppa did everything he could to be the loving, indulgent father to my mum and her brother that Zara wasn't to him and his siblings. Not to mention being a loving and indulgent grandfather to my brother and to me.

Mark and Amelia's marriage certificate from 1850 gave me a few clues which I could use to see if I could trace the origins of our Franklin name. Mark's father is named as Zorach Franklin, who died before his son got married. To try and push further back into history, I investigated the 1841 census. There was Mark, a clothes renovator in his twenties, living in New Castle Street in Spitalfields – just a short distance from the Tenter Ground. In the same house was the slightly older Jacob Franklin (Mark's brother, I assumed) and the Solomons family – Maurice, Charlotte and their three children. The given name of the Solomons' young son, only 9 months old? Zarah.

In Ashkenazi Jewish tradition, children are often named for a relation who has recently passed away. This gave me the tantalising possibility that Zorach died between 1837 (from when all births, marriages and deaths in England and Wales were registered) and 1840 (when young Zarah Solomons was born). This was before the internet, so the search had to be done in person at St. Catherine's House in Aldwych by poring through volumes of indexes, but it proved fruitful. Zorach (spelled Zarah on the certificate) Franklin died on 12th February 1840 at 18 Castle Alley in Spitalfields. What I wasn't expecting was his age at death, suggesting that he was born as early as 1762 or 1763. This suggested that he was well into his fifties when he fathered Mark – strangely similar to his grandson and namesake Zara, who fathered my Poppa at the age of fifty-two. I had only gone back three generations from my grandfather and I was already in the mid-eighteenth century; Zorach was born before the US Declaration of Independence, before the French Revolution and before Captain Cook landed in Australia.

The Solomons family, with whom Mark was living in 1841, also gave me some further clues. By searching through synagogue records (back to the Mormons again to see the originals, although the details are now available at the much-appreciated volunteer website www.synagoguescribes.com), I was able to find the record of Maurice and Charlotte's wedding at the Great Synagogue in Duke's Place. The names weren't a perfect fit – Mordecai Solomon was the groom, and the bride was named as Simme Franklin. Simme's Hebrew name was Simcha, but there was more – it reads *Simcha Bat Zorach Halevi*. Simcha, daughter of Zorach the Levite. The Levite! This was something of which I had no inkling of at all. The Franklins are Levites!

While Jewish status is traditionally passed through the maternal line, the 'tribes' within the Jewish community, such as they still exist, are patrilineal. As far as I knew, all the branches of my family were of no specific tribe, with a status described as simply *Yisroel* (Israelite). Those who are not common Israelites are of two types – the priestly class of *Kohanim* (associated with the surname Cohen) who claim descent from Moses's brother Aaron, and the slightly less exclusive but nevertheless high-status Levites, claiming descent from the rest of the tribe of Levi who were not *Kohanim*. This discovery meant that I could tell Mum that she is a *Bat Levi* – daughter of a Levite – which made her feel extra special for at least an hour or two, until she realised that the one tangible consequence of being a *Bat Levi* would only have mattered several decades earlier when her first son (my brother) was born.

So Zorach, the old porter born in the 1760s, was actually Zorach Halevi. My next find was another marriage record, but this time in Hebrew only. On 6th August 1809 at the New Synagogue in London – the same synagogue where Mark was married 41 years later - a Zorach Halevi married a bride named 'Hendele', and this time we can see Zorach's father's name; *Eliezer Behr Halevi*.

That was where the trail ran cold for a decade or more, until 2010 when I made one last attempt to find a Dutch connection. By chasing down every appearance of the name Zorach in the available records, I found something. Zorach wasn't in Amsterdam himself, but in 1793 his brother got married there. The "pre-nup" (the *Tenaim Acharonim* in Hebrew, which translates as 'final conditions') associated with traditional Jewish marriages gives the names of the groom's brothers, in accordance with Deuteronomy chapter 25 and the practice of Levirate marriage – so Zorach is named, although he is recorded as not having been present. Zorach's father is named once again, but this time with more detail: great swirls of Hebrew script name him as *Eliezer Behr* **Fiorda** *Fraenkel*. It was that word 'Fiorda' which changed everything I thought I knew about the origins of the Franklins.

With the exception of a few earlier ancestors who really are just names and dates without (alas) more detail than that, Jacob "Koppel" Fraenkel (1600-1670) is where my Franklin family story begins. Koppel (the German/Yiddish diminutive of Jacob) is, in a number of sources, identified very clearly as "the richest Jew in Vienna". Which naturally raises two questions – one, where did all the money come from? And two, where did it go? (There is of course a third question – is there any way of getting any of it back – but I've had to conclude that the answer to that one is in the negative).

Starting with question one, it is fairly clear what the major source of Koppel's wealth was. Unsurprisingly for a rich Jew of the time, Koppel was a moneylender – or more specifically, a pawnbroker - but with a very notable clientele. Most significantly (to the family member who later briefly chronicled Koppel's life, at least), he bankrolled no less a figure than George Ducas, the exiled Voivode of Moldovia, who had come to Vienna to try and win his throne back. So for a while at least, it appears that Koppel was holding on to a set of genuine crown jewels, thanks to his ability to come up with ready cash in the amounts necessary to fund an attempt to retake a medium-sized Balkan principality.

Whether he started out rich is an unknown – he was born around 1600 (his age at his death is given as 70, but probably more in a biblical "the life of man is three score years and ten" sense than any accurate assessment of his birthdate; nearly everyone seemed to die at 70 in Jewish 17th century Vienna) in the obscure town of Baiersdorf in Franconia – hence "Fraenkel". Or at least, that makes as much sense as a derivation of his surname as any other suggestion. Of the possible reasons for moving to Vienna, top of the list would probably have to be the fact that in 1632 Baiersdorf was mostly destroyed by marauding armies in the horrific Thirty Years' War, which raged across Central Europe from 1618 onwards. Unlike the Hundred Years' War, this war did last for the length of time its name suggests – which is little comfort to the 30% or more of the population of Germany who were slaughtered in the conflict. By 1648 all sides were exhausted and agreed to stop fighting if only because there was so little left to fight over. Baiersdorf seems to have got it from both sides in 1632, being sacked by both the Protestant Swedish forces (who were in Bavaria largely thanks to King Gustavus Adolphus' oversized ego) and those of the Catholic Emperor.

What we do know is that by the 1640s this Jacob from Franconia, now known as Koppel Fraenkel, was flourishing in Vienna and establishing a family. Like generations of wealthy Jews before and since who have wanted to be remembered as patrons of scholarship and piety, he opened his house to Talmudic scholars and married two of his daughters to highly regarded rabbis who went so far as to take Koppel's surname. However, his grandsons through of one of his sons-in-law weren't quite as studious as Koppel might have wanted, in terms of his hopes for the memory of the Fraenkel name; they went on to become somewhat infamous 'Court Jews' who spent much of their later lives getting in and out of prison, accused of such crimes as treason against the Margrave of Brandenburg-Onoholzbach (I'm not making this up) in the case of one brother, and Kabbalistic sorcery and blasphemy in the case of the other.

In 1651, a financial census reports Koppel's net worth at over 9000 florins – a huge amount by the standards of the day. This was a man with the ear of the Hapsburg Emperor himself. Money talked, but only up to a point. As the 1660s went on, anti-Jewish sentiment increased in Vienna. Perhaps Koppel himself was a source of envy and resentment. Whipped up by the church and members of the royal family (including the Spanish-born Empress Margaret Theresa, who blamed the Jews for her two sons dying young), pressure grew to expel the community from the capital city. Koppel's last few years would have been anxious ones – but with an eye to the future, as it seems that he (or at least his sons, who were probably acting with some guidance from the canny old pawnbroker) did what could be done to mitigate the situation. The family had marriage connections in the town of Fürth back in Franconia, known in Yiddish as *Fiorda*; given that Koppel's sons and grandsons are recorded as community leaders in Fürth and the surrounding communities over the next 50 years or so, at least enough wealth must have been moved out of Vienna to avoid penury.

In April 1670, Koppel died and was buried in the Jewish cemetery in Vienna. Just a few months earlier – perhaps this was what finished him off – the Emperor Leopold I (whose nickname, I'm delighted to report, was 'Leopold the Ugly'. Look at a coin of his, you'll understand why straight away) issued the order for the expulsion of the Vienna Jewish community. They had just a few weeks left to be gone from the city.

Koppel's physical remains, nevertheless, weren't going anywhere. His two sons and one son-in-law, who appear to have acted as the community's voice at court, had arranged for the cemetery to be protected – at considerable cost. Koppel's wealth (possibly still including the crown jewels of Moldovia) was keeping him, and the rest of the Jews buried in Vienna, safe. So effective was this that in 1912, when Bernard Wachstein, the librarian of the old Vienna community, recorded the gravestones in the old cemetery, all of those from Koppel's day – including that of Koppel himself – we all there, undisturbed and legible, ready to be photographed and transcribed. Sadly, the cemetery didn't survive the subsequent depredations of the twentieth century, but at least Koppel's wealth - and his children's efforts – have allowed the photographic image of his tombstone to survive to this day.

The generations between Koppel the Viennese financier and Zorach the East End porter are filled with the leaders and power brokers of the Fürth Jewish community. Koppel's son David Isaac Seckel Fraenkel put his name to a number of new buildings and books, as well as hosting famous rabbis and bringing up six sons to follow him as leaders of the community. His third son Barmann was clearly something of a child prodigy, appointed *Darshan* (Preacher) of the community at just seventeen. At twenty-four, he was elected as Chief Rabbi of Ansbach and Schnaitach. Not everyone loved him though; it is recorded that he was never the Rabbi of Fürth thanks to opposition from his cousin (and Court Jew) Elkan.

Barmann's older brother Jakob Josef was Zorach's grandfather. Born in Vienna, he appears to have been less remarkable than his precocious younger brother. Nevertheless, he can be found in 1716 in the *Schutzgeld* list from Fürth. *Schutzgeld* literally means 'protection money' – the tax which Jews had to pay to maintain their status as *Schutzjuden*, or 'protected Jews'. Jakob Josef paid four florins for the right to live in Fürth (based on the value of the gold in the coins, around £500 in today's money). He was the *Parnass* – what would now be known as the Synagogue Chairman, or in more vernacular Yiddish a *Gantzer Macher* (bigshot). An illustration from a prayer book published in Fürth in 1738 shows an elder of the community lighting a menorah beside the words of the *Al-HaNissim* prayer said on the festival of Chanukah. I wonder if that image, cartoonish as it is, might be a representation of Jakob Josef; well-dressed, full-bearded and solemnly celebrating a festival on behalf of 'his' community.

Head of the community he may have been, but Jakob Josef wouldn't make it very far past 1738. He died on 1st March 1740 aged 73. Unlike his father, he only had a single son who survived him – Eleazar Barmann Fraenkel, born in 1722 when Jakob Josef was already in his fifties. All we know about Eleazar is births and deaths – the births of his seven children, the early deaths of three of them, and then Eleazar's own death. In a strange coincidence, he died twenty years to the day after his father – on 1st March 1760, at only thirty-seven years of age. His wife Esther was left with four children. The youngest of these was not yet three months old when Eleazar died, having been born on 3rd December 1759 and given the Yiddish name Serach – or in Hebrew, Zorach.

After Eliezer's death, his branch of the family disappear from the records in Fürth. I can't help wondering if there was some reason why Eliezer and his children weren't the leaders of the community – the *Gantzer Machers* – that the rest of the Fraenkels continued to be.

Perhaps Eliezer just wasn't interested in community leadership and the need to maintain status and respectability? Maybe he took a bride that the Fraenkel family disapproved of? What we do know is that eighty years after Eliezer's death, Serach Fraenkel HaLevi of Fürth had become Zarah Franklin of Whitechapel. He passed away in one of the poorest and meanest parts of the East End of London, his occupation described simply as 'porter' on his death certificate and his age given as 77. His three surviving children were living in a crowded tenement a short distance away, the two sons living in the household of his daughter and her husband and children.

Zorach must have settled in London at some point before 1809 (the date of his marriage to Hendele at the New Synagogue). Of that period, the years from 1793 onwards were years of almost continuous war between Britain and Europe, as first Revolutionary France and then Napoleon tried to dominate the continent. It therefore seems likely that Zorach was already in England when his brother was getting married in Amsterdam in 1793. What made him move from the town where his family were at the top of the social hierarchy to a new country where his children would grow up in poverty, we simply do not know. The Fraenkel/Franklin story, where I thought I would find nothing but unremarkable Dutch cigar makers, is instead a riches-to-rags tale - from the richest Jew in Vienna to the humblest corner of Spitalfields.

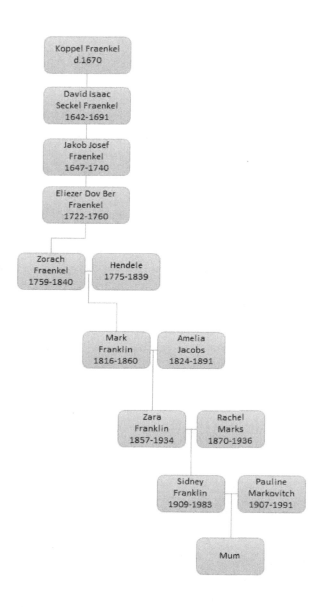

My great-grandfather Zara (Charlie) Franklin, 1857-1934

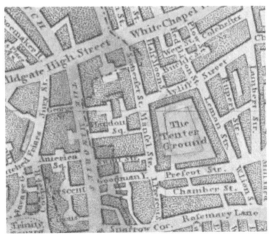

The Tenter Ground in Spitalfields before it was built over, from an 1817 map. Source: Lionel Pincus and Princess Firyal Map Division, The New York Public Library. (1817). "Laurie and Whittle's New map of London with its environs, &c. Including the Recent Improvements".

Cigar Manufacturing at Salmon and Gluckstein Ltd., 1902 – the kind of factory in which Zara worked (image courtesy of Jewish Museum London)

My great-great grandfather Mark Franklin, 1816-1860

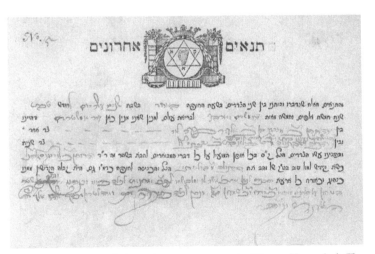

Copy of death certificate of Zarah Franklin, February 1840 - born Serach Fraenkel in 1759 (Crown Copyright)

The 'Tnaim Acharonim' (marriage pre-contract) of Isaac Fraenkel (Zorach's brother), 1793; the document that gave me the connection to the Fraenkel family of Fürth. (Image courtesy of Amsterdam City Archives)

The gravestone of Koppel Fraenkel in Vienna, as recorded in 1912 by community librarian Bernard Wachstein

Image from a Fürth prayerbook of 1738, showing a member of the community lighting the Menorah (Image courtesy of the National Library of Israel)

4 The Surname with No Vowels

Moishe was nineteen and bored. He and his father were inside the Town Hall – the largest building in Rawa other than the church and the castle – but even that became tedious after the first hour. They had now been waiting in line for over four hours, and Moishe had almost finished the few provisions in his bag which were meant to last the whole day. There was nothing to look at here – no items for sale, and worst of all no pretty town girls for his eyes to appreciate. The day was not going the way he had planned.

The others in the queue at the Town Hall were like them; inhabitants of Rawa's "Jews' Town" – now called the *Juden-Stadt* - and Jews from the villages in the surrounding countryside. All men, some with their sons. Moishe knew a few of them by sight, but had exhausted any small talk a long time ago. His father knew most of them through business, although he hadn't been in the area for very long. He also wasn't the most sociable of men, preferring to keep himself to himself most of the time. Finally, they found themselves at the front of the queue with only a door in front of them.

Moishe's father stiffened with anxiety. The son was aware that this was an appointment which his father had dreaded; any interaction with the authorities carried an element of risk for Jews. Moishe took some comfort in the fact that the Jews he saw walking back out of the door seemed none the worse for it. It was then that Moishe noticed the paper pinned to the door at eye level, written in German and Polish. He struggled to read it, being used to the Hebrew characters of the Yiddish language. But one word caught his attention, despite its length and complexity. It was the largest word on the notice: GENERALJUDENREGLEMENT. That was the reason why they were there. Like all the Jews in the newly created Administrative District of Rawa, they had been summoned to be registered in the interests of the area's new overlords – the Kingdom of Prussia.

And not just registered, but also named. This didn't bother Moishe very much at all – he had a name already, and if he needed to be distinguished from any other Moishes (and there were plenty) he simply used his father's name as a patronymic. So what if some official wrote down another name for him? He'd never use it. Besides, who knew how long the Prussians would be in charge? Maybe soon things would be back to the way they always used to be, in a Polish Poland where the Jews got on with their own business without needing any extra names.

The door opened, and a uniformed assistant about the same age as Moishe (but seemingly twice as tall) gestured with his head that the next in line should enter. Moishe's father woke instantly from his reverie, picked up Moishe's bag, shoved it into his son's arms and walked nervously through the door with Moishe following awkwardly while struggling to place the strap of his bag over his head in the way his mother had told him to do around strangers.

The room beyond the door was simple enough, and dominated by a large, polished desk behind which sat a tired-looking Prussian officer, his pince-nez glasses up on his forehead as he squeezed the bridge of his nose and sighed. Standing to the side was a clerk in drab civilian clothes, poised to help the officer when needed. It was the clerk who addressed Moishe's father first, in Polish.

"Stand in front of the Registrar and speak clearly please. State your name."

"Please sir, I am Ksyl ben Anszel."

The clerk scribbled quickly, then continued. "Your occupation and place of residence?"

Ksyl's Polish was broken, but just good enough to respond to the clerk. "I live here, in the Jews' Town. House number fifty-one, although we haven't been in Rawa for that long. And I'm a tailor. Well, most of the time. Sometimes I sell cloth, or other goods…"

"Enough," interjected the Registrar wearily from behind his desk, holding his hand up to indicate that the Jew in front of him should be quiet. The clerk translated Ksyl's answer for him, after which the Prussian nodded and spoke again.

"Not always a tailor, then. So, not *Schneider*. In any case, I've registered too many Schneiders already today."

The Registrar spoke in the educated German of Berlin – related to the Yiddish which Moishe and his father spoke as their mother tongue or *mame-loshn*, but not close enough to enable Moishe's father to catch what he was saying. He looked at the two Jews, replaced his spectacles on his nose, and peered at Moishe and Ksyl again.

"Anton," he said to the clerk, "what name for these two?"

The clerk sighed, and addressed Moishe's father again.

"How long have you lived in Rawa?"

"Oh, not long, sir. We moved here just a few years ago from Lewartow."

The clerk translated again for the Registrar. Moishe really didn't like not being able to understand most of what was being said. He could speak Yiddish, some Hebrew and virtually no Polish at all. This would have to change, he promised himself.

"I suppose we could use the fact that they're newcomers to these parts," the clerk said to the Registrar in German, "so what about *Neumann*?"

"No, I don't think that these two are right for a German name if they've come from east of here. I think they need something a little more… exotic, perhaps."

The Registrar then addressed Moishe's father in slow, overpronounced German, as if talking to a child.

"How – do – you – feel – about – a – POLISH – surname?"

Ksyl recognised the one word which the Registrar had stressed. "Poylisher, ya!" he replied encouragingly, not wanting to cause any offence.

"Good!" announced the Registrar. "Anton, what's the Polish equivalent of Neumann?"

"Well, I suppose it's *Przybysz*, sir. It can mean stranger, visitor, alien, newcomer..."

"Right then, done. Get it written down and tell them what their new name is."

The clerk scribbled again for a while in his book, and then on a separate slip of paper which he handed to Ksyl, with a verbal explanation – in Polish, of course. "This is your name now. You are Ksyl Przybysz, and your wife and children will use that surname on all official and legal documents from now on. You are now registered as a Jewish inhabitant of South Prussia, with rights and duties under the laws of the Kingdom of Prussia. Go home, and learn how to write your new name."

That was that. The nineteen-year-old who walked out of the Town Hall a few minutes later was now Moishe Przybysz.

The story above is of course an imagined account of what might have happened at some point in the years between 1795 and 1807, during which time Rawa Mazowiecka was under Prussian rule. It was almost certainly during that period that my father's family would have been given the surname with no vowels – Przybysz – which I was told was lost. There was a Ksyl ben Anszel who came to Rawa from Lubartow, a town not far from the city of Lublin in the Eastern part of Poland – although Ksyl would have known it by its Yiddish name of Lewartow. It's entirely possible that Ksyl left Lubartow after a major fire there in 1792 and headed west to settle in Rawa, where a small Jewish community of tailors, craftsmen and merchants was starting to grow.

The reason that so much of this is guesswork is that it was only at the turn of the nineteenth century – the years either side of 1800 – that Jews started to be treated as subjects of the state in the same way as their Christian neighbours. The Enlightenment of the 1700s had seen slow and gradual change, but the French Revolution turbocharged the new way in which Jews were seen across Europe. In 1797 Prussia's *General-Juden-Reglement für Süd- und Neu-Ostpreussen* required all Jews now under Prussian rule (including Ksyl and his teenage son Moishe) to make themselves known to the new authorities, and take surnames rather than relying on patronymics. Then in 1807, an agent of change arrived who would upset the status quo wherever he went; the Emperor Napoleon. After defeating the Austrians, Prussians and Russians in turn, Napoleon found himself taking up the cause of Poland, thanks in no small measure to the beguiling (and extremely patriotic) charms of his new mistress Marie Walewska. The territories taken by Prussia a few years earlier were to be reorganised as the Grand Duchy of Warsaw, run on French Revolutionary principles. Well, almost. There was probably a little more *Liberté*, *Egalité* and *Fraternité* than before in Rawa, but only as far as it suited French interests.

What it did mean is that from 1807, civil registers of vital records were kept across the Grand Duchy in a format which survived for over a hundred years, even if the Grand Duchy itself didn't last beyond 1813. And these records of births, marriages and deaths applied to everyone regardless of religion. So in a record from Rawa written on 5th July 1809, the name Przybysz appears for the first time in an event that I can definitely link to my own family history. Sadly, this was Ksyl reporting the death of his teenaged daughter Frommet. He next appears in 1814 as a witness to the birth of a grandchild. Both these records have his signature, in Yiddish script (cursive Hebrew letters), telling us how he would have pronounced his own name: "Kusiel Pshybish."

Ksyl's next appearance is as the subject of a record, rather than as a witness or informant. On 26th May 1821, he passed away at home in the Jewish Quarter of Rawa, well into his sixties. This is where we see him described as *rod em z Lewartowa Miasta* – a native of the town of Lubartow. His death record goes on to name his surviving children, starting with his firstborn son 'Moyzes' – or in Yiddish, Moishe.

In my imagined account of how the name Przybysz came to be ours, I suggested that Moishe was frustrated by the communication problems faced by his father as a result of living in an insular community, speaking in Yiddish and praying in Hebrew. Whatever the reason, Moishe didn't follow his father into what their descendants in twentieth-century London would call "the *schmutta* business". His first appearance in the surviving vital records is in 1810, when the Grand Duchy of Warsaw was at its peak – but this record is not from Rawa.

The tiny village of Wilcze Piętki is 25km east of Rawa in the middle of an expanse of flat, featureless farmland south-west of Warsaw. In neat, careful script, it was the parish priest of the nearest town who recorded that the Jew Mosiek Przybysz made the 10km journey from Wilcze Piętki to Biala Rawska to register the death of his daughter Ryfka. The wording of the document is as informative as it is tragic, giving a couple of tantalising hints about Moishe's life: "*The Jew Moszek Przybysz the Lessee, in Wilcze Piętki residing... testified that on the tenth of the month in this year, at the first hour of night, passed away his daughter named Ryfka, born of Taube his wife aged 30, who completed her life aged two in Wilcze Piętki at the Inn with her parents.*"

Moishe was getting away from the static town life of his father. Not only was he living in a rural hamlet that did not even have its own church or priest, but this record also tells us that he was the innkeeper of the place. It's entirely possible that Moishe and his wife Taube were, to coin a phrase, "the only Jews in the village". And they were the pub landlord and landlady!

While Jews and pubs might not be two things that automatically get put together in contemporary minds, a great deal of nineteenth century inns across rural Poland were run by Jews under the system of *arenda* or leaseholding. In simple terms, the land was owned by the nobility, but what the nobility really wanted was not what the land directly produced. Rather than bushels of wheat or gallons of milk,

50

the landowners preferred to have ready cash. The best way to make that happen was to lease the land to people who could turn wheat, wood, cattle and vegetables into coins. And the people who could do that most effectively were very often Jews.

The most effective means of turning agricultural produce into cash was through holding the monopoly rights over the sale of alcohol in the area – the *propinacja*. While Jews did not have the legal right to own land, they were able to take ownership of the *propinacja* through paying a hefty fee to the landowner. The noble Polish landowner got a lump sum up front, and the Jewish lessee – known as the *arendarz* – took over the village inn. No less an authority than the YIVO Encyclopaedia of Jews in Eastern Europe suggests that the success of Jews in holding positions as innkeepers *"was a result of several factors: modest drinking habits, relatively advanced literacy and mathematical knowledge, but above all their ability to pay in advance."*

To be a successful innkeeper, Moishe must have become fluent in Polish, and fully conversant in the lives of his non-Jewish clientele. The rural inn was the hub of social and economic life in villages like Wilcze Piętki. It would have also acted as a local shop and pawnbroker, where Moishe and Taube would be the people who took what little money the local peasants had in exchange for imported luxuries, as well as being the people who provided them with money on credit against the items they might pawn. Inevitably, this could cause tensions between Jewish innkeepers and the local community. Moishe would need to have significant people management skills to navigate his relationships with the peasants whom he served, not to mention the landowner whom he paid for his lease. The character of the Jewish innkeeper makes a number of appearances in nineteenth-century Polish literature – not always kindly, but not always as the villain either. I would hope that Moishe was not seen as the bad guy by the villagers of Wilcze Piętki.

Eight years later, Moishe and Taube had moved to another tiny village, where another child of theirs died young. Nowy Dwór is 12km north of Rawa Mazowiecka, and about 20km as the crow flies from Wilcze Piętki. This was also a place too small to have its own priest, so deaths had to be registered somewhere else. The nearest such place was the wooden parish church of Saints Simon and Tadeusz Jude in Stara Rawa. This time it was a son's passing which Moishe had the sad task of registering – Herszek Przybysz, just three years old. Moishe is no longer described an innkeeper; he is now a *komornik*, which means bailiff or debt collector. From being the genial provider of drink, food and gossip in one village, it seems that the Przybyszs may have been seen rather differently in the next village in which they settled. Moishe's was now the face the locals didn't want to see.

As far as we know, Moishe and Taube remained childless for five more years after Herszek's death. Two years after Moishe's father Ksyl had died, his mother Pessa passed away in March 1823 in the same house where her husband had done so. The witnesses named on Ksyl's death record are Pessa herself, and Berek Fuks, another tailor in Rawa. On Pessa's death record, both witnesses are family members – Moishe's younger brother Chaym, and his brother in law Wolf Szer (married to Moishe's sister Chaya). But as for Moishe, he was nowhere to be seen. He was still living the rural village life away from the town where his parents had lived out their final years.

Five months after his mother died, Moishe and Taube were finally able to celebrate a birth – this time of a child who would survive to adulthood. Once again, they were living in a place so small that they had to register the child in the nearest settlement large enough to have a parish priest. That settlement was the village of Krzemienica, 11km south of Rawa and set in another expanse of flat, featureless farmland almost indistinguishable from the land around Moishe's previous residences. Walking or riding a further 5km south of Krzemienica would get you to a place called Stanislawow. This is another of those points where things could get confusing - there are more than forty villages called Stanislawow across Poland, so making sure that you're looking at the right one is not always a sure thing. Most of these Stanislawows have a suffix or nickname to distinguish them from other villages of the same name, but not the Stanislawow near Krzemienica. Perhaps it was so small and unremarkable that it didn't even merit any extra name. Even today on Google Streetview, all that can be seen are a few buildings with not even a sign on the road to tell someone that they're driving through a named location.

Moishe now has another occupation to add to his resumé: *Okupnik*. He was a tenant farmer – in all likelihood *the* tenant farmer in Stanislawow – residing "on the farm" (*na gospodarcturic zamieszkaly*) with Tauba. This suggests that he was a leaseholder again, paying the local landowner for the right to live on the farm and convert its agricultural produce into cash – although whether Moishe and Tauba actually put in the hours behind a plough, or milking the cows, is more doubtful. The child whose birth was recorded in this entry was a boy, and the name given could not have been a difficult choice; in line with Ashkenazi Jewish tradition, Moishe named his son after a male relative who had recently passed away – his own father Ksyl. The boy was named Kisiel.

Three years later, Moishe was registering another birth, but things in this part of Poland were changing. Napoleon had brought with the idea that even Jews could be equal citizens, so the life events of Jews and Gentiles were registered together in the Grand Duchy of Warsaw. This continued for a while, but after Napoleon's defeat in 1814 Rawa and the area around it were part of the Kingdom of Congress Poland – the king in this case being the Tsar of Russia. As the Russians started to tighten their grip on Poland, it was decreed that Jewish births, marriages and deaths should be kept separate from those of other denominations. That was why Moishe had to travel all the way to Rawa to register the birth of his daughter Pessa, born in 1826. The Przybyszs were still living on the farm in Stanislawow, although Moishe's occupation in agriculture is prefaced by the Polish word *dawniej* (formerly). He was now getting close to fifty years old; perhaps he no longer needed to work himself, and simply oversaw the labourers as they produced the harvests which allowed him to pay the leasehold on the farm? I'd like to think that this was the case and that he and Tauba (who was more than a decade younger than him – maybe she was doing all the work so that Moishe could sit on his backside; she wouldn't have been the first or the last Jewish wife do have done so, I'm sure) were able to enjoy time with their young children in semi-retirement.

The two of them were still living in Stanislawow eighteen years later, when their son Kisiel got married. His intended was from Wyśmierzyce, 50 km to the east. Kisiel's nearest big town with a synagogue that could host such a celebration was Rawa, while for his bride-to-be that location would be the town of Przytyk. The marriage banns were declared in both towns – perhaps while the two families debated where the wedding would take place. In the end, Moishe (now in his sixties) and Taube had to *schlep* across central Poland – although whether they were upset at having to make the journey, or delighted that the bride's family were hosting and therefore paying for most of the event, we can only guess. On 30th December 1844, Kisiel married Malka Rotbard, the daughter of butcher Szmul and his wife Sura. Twenty-one-year-old Kisiel had taken up the profession of the grandfather for whom who had been named, as a *krawiec* – a tailor.

Moishe passed away in 1848, at almost seventy years of age. The following year, Kisiel named a newborn son for his father, and for the older brother that he never got to meet: Mosiek Hersz. Eagle-eyed readers will recall that this was the birth record which I first found while searching for my great-grandfather Myer. The patronymic on Myer's gravestone – which I read as "Katriel" – should have been Kisiel (a rookie error on my part; I was following the Israeli pronunciation which I had been taught, where the Hebrew letter Tav is always pronounced as a "t" – but the Ashenazi tradition of my forebears is to pronounce it as an "s"). Mosiek Hersz was an older brother of Myer. My direct paternal ancestral line starts with Ksyl's father Anszel and runs down the generations through Ksyl, Moishe, Kisiel, Myer and Morry to my dad.

It's hard not to like Moishe. A tailor's son, born in one town and taken to another on the other side of Poland, he was given the name "newcomer" without asking for it. But I would argue that his subsequent career moving from hamlet to hamlet around Rawa, living and working closely with the non-Jewish population in popular and less popular roles, meant that he really 'owned' the name Przybysz rather than being embarrassed by it. He wasn't afraid of being the newcomer, the stranger, the outsider, the one in a different situation from those around him. Perhaps there is a certain irony in the fact that his son and grandson stayed put in Rawa. It was the generation after that – my grandpa's generation – who, as they shed the name Przybysz to become Beaches, were once again newcomers.

I was told that our original family surname was a mystery, and that all traces of those who carried it were likewise lost. Thankfully, that wasn't the case - and characters like Moishe the itinerant village innkeeper (amongst the other roles he played) have emerged from the dry records, living complex lives in a diverse and changing multicultural society rather than the fixed, unchanging and inward-looking *shtetl* of popular imagination.

It's time to honour Moishe's memory. I'm off to the pub.

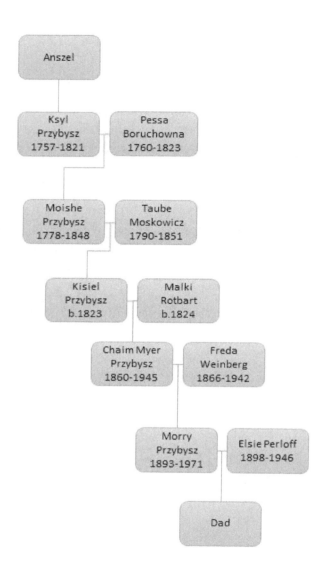

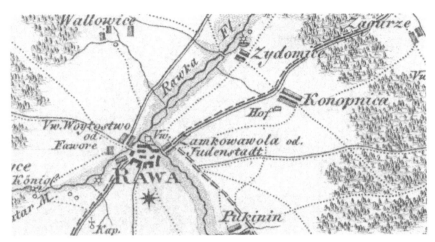

Detail from an 1803 Prussian map of Rawa Mazowiecka, showing the location of the 'Judenstadt' (Source: David Rumsey Map Collection, David Rumsey Map Center, Stanford Libraries)

Death record of Moishe's two-year-old daughter Ryfka in the village of Wilcze Pietki, 10th June 1810 (image courtesy of the Polish State Archives in Warsaw, Grodzisk Mazowiecki branch)

Birth record of Moishe's son Kisiel Przybysz, 16th August 1823 (image courtesy of the Polish State Archives in Warsaw, Grodzisk Mazowiecki branch)

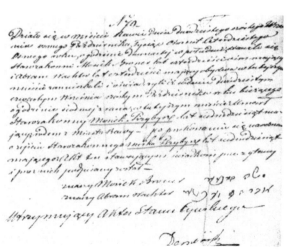

Death record of Moishe Przybysz aged 70, 6th October 1848 (image courtesy of the Polish State Archives in Warsaw, Grodzisk Mazowiecki branch)

5 My Litvak Great-Grandpa

Of course, I married above my station. My family tend to be so self-deprecating that anyone marrying into the Beaches is told (jokingly, I hope) that they should know they're taking a downwards step in social status by associating with us. My wife traces her descent on her mother's side from a family of influential ladies' fashion retailers, with shops in multiple locations including Central London (my in-laws have a picture of the family on the balcony of their shop on Oxford Street, cheering as the coronation procession went by in 1953). As for her father's side – well, as she is so often fond of reminding me, that's where true Jewish nobility can be found. Many a disagreement has been settled by my wife pulling rank as a direct descendant of Rabbi Eliyahu ben Shlomo Zalman, the Gaon of Vilna. This is someone described as "one of the most influential rabbinic authorities since the Middle Ages"; this is someone who appeared on a 10-Euro coin in 2020, the first and only Euro coin to have Hebrew letters on it; this is someone commonly referred to in Hebrew as *ha-Gaon ha-Chasid mi-Vilna*, "the pious genius from Vilnius". This is someone important. And if that wasn't enough, the Vilna Gaon is reputed to have been descended from King David himself. I truly did marry royalty.

The nearest I could get to the Vilna Gaon was that I did at least have one great-grandparent whom I knew to be a *Litvak* – a Jew from Lithuania. Within the Ashkenazi world, it's not uncommon for

Litvaks to consider themselves, if not royalty, at least not quite as common and uncouth as the *Poliaks* with whom they were often lumped. If my ancestry didn't include the Vilna Gaon himself, it did at least include some of the educated, scholarly Lithuanian Jews who formed his congregation.

The great-grandparent in question was Marks Markovitch, well-remembered by my mum as her kindly old grandfather living down in Bournemouth until his death in 1958. Only a couple of years earlier he was living in Gransden Avenue, off Mare Street in Hackney – the same address where he and his family had been for over three decades, and the house where my Nanna (born Pauline Markovitch) grew up. This is the address which appears in a document of which Marks was extremely proud; his Certificate of Naturalization, registered at the Home Office on 26th November 1919. Marks took the Oath of Allegiance to His Majesty King George the Fifth and His Heirs and Successors, and became a British Subject.

That certificate also gives his date and place of birth – 1st September 1877 in Kovno, Russia. Although it was part of the Russian Empire in 1877, the city of Kovno (now known by its Lithuanian name, Kaunas) is very definitely in Lithuania; as Marks was taking his oath, the city was the location of the government of the brand new Republic of Lithuania, setting itself up as the first independent Lithuanian state since 1569 as the empires that existed up to the First World War collapsed into chaos. Kovno/Kaunas became the capital of Lithuania throughout the inter-war period, although it was officially the temporary capital while Vilnius was under Polish rule until 1939.

The 1891 England & Wales census allowed me to date more specifically when Marks arrived in England from his Lithuanian birthplace. He is one of only two siblings born abroad – the rest of the Markovitch brothers and sisters are recorded as born in London. At 6 Eckersley Street Bethnal Green, Marks' father Abraham is listed as a tailor's presser aged 40, and his mother Leah is 37. Betsy the oldest child is 16, then Marks is a 13-year-old apprentice (although other records suggest that he was still at school at the time) – all four of them with the non-specific birthplace of *Russia, Poland*. The other siblings, starting with Lazarus aged 9, were all born in London. Two further salient facts emerged from more research: Lazarus was born on 22nd Feb 1882, and there was no sign of the family in the 1881 England & Wales census which was taken on 3rd April. While no specific record of their arrival has yet been found, I can say that the Markovitch family – Abraham, Leah, Betsy and a three- or four-year-old Marks – must have arrived in the UK between April 1881 and February 1882.

There's no surprise at all that this should be the window within which they would have fled the Russian Empire. The year 1881 saw the start of the most brutal period of pogroms in the history of the Jews of the Russian Empire – and the start of mass emigration of Jews from Poland. Lithuania, Belarus and Ukraine to Western Europe and North America. On 13th March 1881, Tsar Alexander II was assassinated in St. Petersburg by a group of nihilist revolutionaries who thought they could bring about a revolution by killing the relatively moderate emperor known as 'Alexander the Liberator'. The event shook the Russian Empire and, as such events often do, strengthened the position of extremists on both sides. When it emerged that one member of the assassins' gang was Jewish by birth, officials took the opportunity to lay the blame on 'agents of foreign influence' – even today a barely concealed code for blaming the Jews. A month after the assassination was Easter, when (even at the best of times) the risk of congregations being swept up into a frenzy of rage against the matzo-baking-with-Christian-blood, messiah-denying, Christ-killing Jews was ever present. The first pogroms happened in present-day Ukraine, around Kherson and Kiev. In Jewish memory, this was the start of the Storms in the South (*ha-sufot ba-negev*) – the worst wave of antisemitic attacks in Eastern Europe since the Khmelnytsky Uprising of 1648-58 saw tens of thousands of Jews massacred by Cossacks.

Lithuania was some distance away from the main focus of the pogroms of 1881-2, but Abraham and Leah would have no doubt heard the reports as more and more tragic news reached them from elsewhere in the Empire. Even this far north, it's entirely possible that the Tsar's assassination had led to ill-feeling and an increase in repression for Jewish communities. In any case, the Markovitches packed up and made their way to a port (probably in the German Empire) from where they could take ship for London. It clearly took them a while to get used to how things were done in the UK; while Lazarus was (according to all the records we have for him) born in London in February 1882, his birth does not seem to have been registered.

New immigrants they may have been, but they were willing to answer their country's call when the time came. Marks' Naturalization Certificate from 1919 has the note "has served in His Majesty's Forces" – even the foreign-born eldest son joined up to serve in the First World War, albeit in the Labour Corps rather than as a front line soldier. At least two of his brothers also served; their military service records show them to be certified as medical grade B2, perhaps as a result of growing up in the not so healthy conditions of Edwardian Bethnal Green. Ironically, their poor health may have been what lengthened their lives, as being B2 put you in the Labour Corps rather than the regiments going over the top.

But before that, Marks needed to be transformed from a Lithuanian immigrant child to an Anglo-Jewish teenager. And there was no better place for that than the Jews' Free School. Founded in 1732, by the time the seven-year-old Marks was enrolled in the school it was located in Bell Lane, in the heart of the Jewish East End. Marks was one of upwards of three thousand pupils in the school, and it was ever growing as more and more Jewish families arrived from the Russian Empire escaping the persecutions of the 1880s. By 1900 it would be the largest school in Europe, with four thousand pupils. Knowing that I have a distant ancestor who was schooled at JFS (as the modern version of the Jews' Free School is now known) is particularly meaningful to me, as I have no small connection with the school myself – in the 1980s as a pupil, in the

1990s as a teacher and most recently in the 2010s as a parent.

The figure whose imposing presence must have dominated Marks' schooling was that of Moses Angel, the headteacher. It is his handwriting which details Marks' admission to the school on 13th April 1885, adding his father's name (Abraham) and home address – 8 Charles Street – as well as a date of birth, although only the month and year (September 1877) are written. Angel was a strict disciplinarian and micromanager, who insisted on keeping records himself throughout his many decades as headmaster. One of the four JFS school houses still bears his name to this day.

Another JFS teacher whom Marks may have known during his time in Bell Lane was not only a teacher, but also a former pupil of the school (JFS has always been a school where a number of students find themselves, like myself, returning there to teach; whether this is because we are so inspired by our teachers that we seek to emulate them, or just that we find ourselves unable to be of any real use anywhere else, it's surely not for me to say). This was Israel Zangwill, who had just earned his Bachelor of Arts degree (with triple honours, *noch*) from the University of London when Marks joined the school. Zangwill went on to become perhaps the most celebrated writer of the Jewish East End, drawing on his experiences in the school and the area around it for his ground-breaking novel *Children of the Ghetto*. Zangwill also has a house at JFS still named for him. Being an alumnus of Zangwill House myself, I have a special affinity with and respect for the author and playwright known as "the Dickens of the Ghetto".

One of the ironies of how JFS has changed, from the school attended by Marks in the 1880s to that attended by my brother and I in the 1980s, is that its key purpose has in many ways been completely reversed. In the days of Moses Angel's headship, the purpose of the school was clear – as Zangwill described in his novel, the JFS school bell could be heard "*summoning its pupils from the reeking courts and alleys, from the garrets and the cellars, calling them to come and be Anglicized.*" Angel saw it as his task to turn immigrant children who could speak only Yiddish and Hebrew into young Englishmen and

Englishwomen, capable of contributing to wider society with a full secular curriculum (as well as a little religious teaching of course). He reserved a particular distaste for Yiddish, *"the most shamelessly corrupt and hybrid jargon ever evolved"* as some referred to it. Of course, not everyone approved; one of Zangwill's characters, in that same novel, laments the approach that Angel was taking:

"'Lessons!' snorted Malka. 'What's the good of lessons? It's English, not Judaism, they teach them in that godless school. I could never read or write anything but Hebrew in all my life; but God be thanked, I have thriven without it. All they teach them in the school is English nonsense. The teachers are a pack of heathens, who eat forbidden things, but the good Yiddishkeit goes to the wall.'"

Fast forward by a century or more, and JFS exists for the opposite reason; now the school teaches Hebrew and *Yiddishkeit* to children who only speak English, rather than the other way around. And yet the school's core purpose is still to try and meet the current needs of the young people of the community, whether that be secular or religious (or both). In some ways, the ultimate aim remains the same; for those leaving JFS to have a strong and well-rounded secular education while still having pride in their Jewish heritage and the knowledge of their religion enabling them to be fully involved and practising Jews – should they choose to follow that path.

For families like the Markovitches, the Jews' Free School would have provided more than just lessons. The school was blessed with donations from the wealthier members of the community, many of whom were eager to do all they could to help Anglicize the unwashed *Poliaks* and *Litvaks* arriving every day and threatening the good name of the upwardly mobile existing community. These donations allowed the school to provide clothes and food for those pupils that needed them – contingent, of course, on them attending their English lessons and progressing towards being good citizens. Marks made such progress; in Moses Angel's careful hand, his ascent through the educational levels was marked with the date of achieving each milestone – Level One in 1887, and a step up each year to Level Four in 1890. There his progress stopped, although his leaving wasn't recorded until 1892 with two levels still remaining to be achieved.

Perhaps the fact that the 1891 census lists Marks as an apprentice rather than a scholar tells us where his attention was focused during those last two years at school; perhaps the family finances meant that those two final levels needed to take a back seat to bringing in a wage.

Having left school at fourteen, Marks was still living at home in 1901 when the census of that year lists him as a Boot Laster. This was quite a skilled task involving the assembly of a boot from the various pre-stitched or cut pieces of iron, wood and leather. The leather needed to be stretched and shaped over a wooden mould to form the upper, and then tacked into place carefully but quickly. Bethnal Green was known as an area specialising in this industry, with a combination of small workshops and large factories. The "where born" column in the 1901 census is again vague for Marks, simply saying "*Russia, NK*" – the NK standing for Not Known.

By the 1911 census we find Marks in Hackney, aged 33 and now married with two daughters and a French Polisher (meaning a furniture finisher, not someone of Franco-Polish origin) who was living with the family and no doubt helping with the rent. The census form – which for the first time, was filled in by the subjects of the census themselves, rather than an enumerator going door to door and asking verbally, shows Marks' occupation as 'Boot Maker', and tells us that he is an employee rather than working for himself. This time, the detail in the Birthplace column is a little more forthcoming. Marks gives his birthplace as "*Sualk, Russia*" – not Kovno. Although there is no such place as Sualk.

Fortunately, a look at the map of the Lithuania and the area around it gives a couple of possible answers as to what Marks was trying to write on his census form. About 120km north of Kaunas is the city of Siauliai, the fourth largest in Lithuania. In the late nineteenth century half the population was Jewish, and it was known for its leather industry – could this be a connection to Marks (and his brothers) entering the shoemaking business? The other possibility was also about 120km away, but this time to the south. The city of

Suwalki also had a significant Jewish population at the time of Marks' birth. But one thing made me slightly uneasy about the possibility that Marks was born there. Suwalki isn't in Lithuania. It's in Poland.

With at least two more well-defined areas to focus on, the search for any Eastern European records that might locate the Markovitches more specifically was on. Any records of Marks' birth remain elusive, but two records emerged from the 1875 indexes of JRI-Poland which looked promising. On November 20th 1875, a baby girl was born called Shayna Marcowicz, to parents Abram and Leah. Nine months and four days earlier, Abram Itsko Marcowicz married Leah Hofmann (Shayna was very definitely a honeymoon baby). Abram and Leah match the names of Marks' parents perfectly, and Shayna's age matches that of Marks' older sister – she may have been born in the *shtetl* as Shayna, but in London she was Betsy. Both of these events registered in the town of Krasnopol, about 15km due east of the town of Suwalki, and part of the Suwalki *Gubernia* (province) between 1867 and 1914.

But where was my great-grandfather's birth? With no sign of it in any other location, the most likely answer is that it was lost. After 1875, the next year for which there are birth records for this town is 1882 – by which time the family were in London. Marks' birth in 1877 is in one of the lost years, but it almost certainly took place in Krasnopol, in the Suwalki province of Russian Poland. The place is still a small village, with a population of just 1300. At most, it would have had only a few hundred Jewish inhabitants in the late nineteenth century. The synagogue building, constructed in 1850, still stands in the form of a general shop which sadly closed for good during the COVID-19 pandemic. The area around Krasnopol was, at the time of Marks' birth, the least economically developed area of Russian Poland, with the lowest levels of agricultural output.

Abraham and Leah's marriage certificate, handwritten in Cyrillic script, is particularly difficult to decipher – but it does confirm that the Markovitches were hardly urbane sophisticates. The 28-year-old Abraham Marcowicz (using the most commonly occurring of the many spellings of the surname in Eastern European records) was a native of Krasnopol, probably not venturing far from the village. His occupation is not given, although in London he was a tailor's presser for two decades. Not a master tailor, but an assistant employed by a self-employed tailor or a clothes-making factory. His parents are named on the record, providing further confirmation that this is the same person. Abraham's gravestone in Edmonton Cemetery names him as *Avraham Yitzchak ben Leib Velvel*, while his father on the marriage record is Lejba Wolf; Velvel is the Yiddish form of Wolf.

Leah's surname was Hofmann (or Gofmann; in Russian G and H are often interchangeable), daughter of Mortchel and Rochla (Mordechai and Rachel) Hofmann. She was a few years younger than Abraham, and from a different village – the wonderfully named Punsk, 15km north of Krasnopol and even closer to the border with Lithuania. Punsk was about the same size as Krasnopol, but it had previously held the status of a town. Just a couple of years before Leah was born there, the inhabitants of poverty-stricken Punsk petitioned the authorities to remove the burdens and duties that came with town status. A survey conducted a few years before that was not exactly bursting with civic pride: "*Punsk... does not deserve to remain in the title of a town. Trade (is) almost completely unknown here... If there is any industry, we can find it abandoned... There is only one street, and it is crooked, leading uphill and deserted. If you consider crafts, these end here with a few clumsy Jewish tailors, shoemakers and clog manufacturers.*" This was the environment into which Leah was born. She was the youngest of her family, and her father Mortchel was a tailor (perhaps one of the 'clumsy Jewish tailors' mentioned in the earlier survey) in his mid-forties when Leah was born. Mortchel was most likely the grandfather for whom Marks Markovitch was named, both having the Hebrew name Mordechai.

Mortchel and Rochel's marriage record from 1833 has survived, adding another village on the Poland/Lithuania border to the list of those with a family connection. Rochel was living with her parents in Smolany, a hamlet even smaller than Punsk or Krasnopol. No population data from the nineteenth century has survived, but over the past 50 years the population of Smolany peaked in the year 2000 at a massive twenty-eight people. Rochel's home may have been a genuine one-horse town, if indeed it had any horses at all. The Punsk records allow the Hoffmans to be traced even further back; Mortchel was born in 1809 (in the Grand Duchy of Warsaw) to Koppel and Szejna, who were both born in the 1770s as the Partitions of Poland-Lithuania were just beginning.

As for taking the Markovitch/Marcowicz story further back, the records from Krasnopol tell us more. In September 1842, Lejba Wolf married Tauba Rochla Chaimowitz (Abraham's parents). Lejba is described as a *wyrobnik* – an unskilled worker or labourer – aged twenty-four. The parents of both bride and groom are named, but the names are all we know about them. The one exception is Abraham's paternal grandfather Lejzor Marcowicz, whose death record survives. He died in July 1860, with his age given as seventy (although, as mentioned in previous chapters, seventy can be a 'go-to' lifespan when the actual age of the deceased is not precisely known). He is also described as a *wyrobnik*. If his age at death is reliable, he would have been born in 1790 – meaning that he was almost certainly born in the Commonwealth of Poland-Lithuania five years before it ceased to exist and all these villages in the Suwalki area came under Prussian rule. Lejzor's father is named – another Mortchel, who was probably the first of the family to officially take the surname Marcowicz (perhaps this Mortchel's father was the original 'Mark' in 'Markovitch'), standing in front of a Prussian official in a similar way that Ksyl Przybysz may have done in Chapter Four.

We knew that the Markovitches weren't rich, but my hope – based on what I had been told – was that this Lithuania-based branch of the family might furnish me with something different compared to the regular *schmuttemachers*, *schleppers* and *schnorrers* of the rural Polish *shtetls*. What I have found has been fascinating, but not what I was hoping or even expecting. The Hoffman and Marcowicz families weren't urbane, or even the slightest bit urban; most surprisingly, they weren't even Lithuanian. Each village to which I tracked them down was tantalisingly close to the Polish-Lithuanian border, but always on the Polish side. Culturally, they may have seen themselves as *Litvaks* and perhaps spoke with a dialect of Yiddish more familiar in Vilna than in Warsaw – but the fact is, they lived in Poland.

Perhaps the most remarkable story in the lives of this side of the family is how successfully mine and Marks' alma mater – the Jews' Free School – did its job. Moses Angel, Israel Zangwill and the rest of the staff were able to make something of a boy born in one of the tiniest, poorest villages in the most remote part of Russian Poland, descended from unskilled workers who lived in even smaller and even poorer villages. JFS turned out a young man who served his adopted country, achieved citizenship and raised a family to the point where he could retire in comfort and live out his final years by the sea as a much-loved grandfather. Not that JFS can take all the credit, of course; no doubt Abraham and Leah had something to do with it, and of course Marks himself. He might not have been a truly '*Litvak*' great-grandpa, but there's certainly a lot to be proud of in his story.

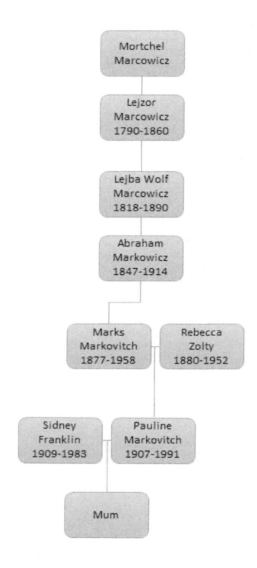

The Vilna Gaon (1720-1797), from whom my wife is directly descended (image from the photographic archive of the Jewish Theological Seminary of America)

Marks Markovitch, my 'Litvak' great-grandfather and JFS alumnus (1877-1958)

Marriage record of Mortchel Hofmann and Rochla Leybowicz from Smolany near Punsk, 3rd December 1833 (image courtesy of the Polish State Archives in Warsaw, Suwalki branch)

71

Abraham Icko Markowicz (1847-1914), who took his family from Krasnopol to London in 1881-2

Leah Markowicz nee Hofmann (1854-1926), born in Punsk – a town with "a few clumsy Jewish tailors, shoemakers and clog manufacturers"

The main entrance of the Jews' Free School in Bell Lane (image courtesy of Jewish Museum London)

6 My Polish Great-Grandma

Jewishness is traditionally matrilineal. In Orthodox Judaism, Jewish status is inherited through the female line, and only after that is any other element of Jewishness (for example, one's priestly status as a *Kohen*) passed down in a patrilineal way. Over countless generations it may have been the men who attended synagogue, studied and prayed, but the real Jewish inheritance is in the home – where throughout history one Jewish mother after another has kept the Shabbat candles lit and the familial Jewish identity alive. For that reason, one line of my ancestry has always been particularly special to me – going back through the female line that gave me my Jewishness; from my own mother back through all the Jewish mothers that I could uncover. The surnames might change in each generation through marriage, but this was perhaps the strongest line of all with each link from mother to daughter.

Not long after I started my family research journey, I was lucky enough to spend some quality time with my Nanna – my mum's mum – to talk about her family history. She would have been eighty-three, and (although we didn't know it at the time) was entering the last year of her life. In keeping with the high standards of research methodology which I practised at the time, the only record I have of that talk is on one single sheet of a memo pad about the size of a playing card. The character she talked about the most was her mother Rebecca, known to the world as Becky; clearly the most important and influential figure in her life. She wasn't entirely sure where Becky was born, but it was somewhere in Poland. Near the German border maybe, but definitely Poland. A little more questioning of other relations on that side of the family gave me a location for where Becky's family had lived – Kalisz, a city in the west of Congress Poland and under Russian rule from 1814 until well after the family moved to England. Becky Zolty, as she was before marrying Marks Markovitch, was my Polish Great-Grandma – my mum's mum's mum. What I wanted to do was look into this female line, and see what stories might be uncovered.

One surprising outcome of my research was that the story of my foremothers, as far back as I have been able to trace, does not start in Poland. It starts a little further west, in what was the Grand Duchy of Posen and part of the Kingdom of Prussia in the 1820s. The earliest direct maternal ancestor I can name is Ester Gutmann, who would have been born around the time that the 1700s became the 1800s. It's not known exactly where she was born, but by the 1820s she was Ester Altmann, and living in Kempen (now called Kępno) under Prussian rule. Ester was the baker's wife, and by the start of the next decade she had at least two daughters – Reizel born in 1826, and Laje in 1830.

An extensive account of Jewish life in Kempen from the early to mid-1800s survives in the archives of the *Jahrbuch fuer juedische Geschichte und Literatur* (Jewish History and Literature Yearbook), held in the University of Frankfurt. For the 1923 volume, Isidore Kasten wrote a 50-page 'Cultural Sketch' of the community as it had been two or three generations earlier. Isidore tells us that there were about 4000 Jews in the town, representing two-thirds of the total population. Kempen was a border town, looking both west to Germany and east to Poland: "*One could breathe Silesian air and enjoy the cleanliness and industry of the farmyards, (but) if one turned… eastward into Poland, the cultural situation was too depressing to be taken in in a glance.*" If he is to be believed, the community was clearly much keener on looking westward. And not just westward to the rest of Germany;

overseas emigration from the slow pace of life in Kempen was an attractive option to the younger Jews of the town. What is particularly interesting, almost comically so, is the description of the preferred destination of these Kempeners; *"there was only one country that interested them; that was England… Commercial Road, Whitechapel, Petticoat Lane."*

The depressing view eastward into Poland would have been an even more depressing one as 1830 turned into 1831. The November 1830 uprising of Polish nationalists against Russian rule was brutally crushed, and in early October 1831 the final remnants of Polish resistance had crossed into Prussia to surrender. At the very end of that year, on 31st December (although Ester probably knew it as the 27th of the Hebrew month of Tevet, a few weeks after Chanukah), her husband – the baker Aron Altmann – died of cholera. One can only hope that the doughnuts he might have baked a few weeks earlier were not infected. As well as having two young daughters, Ester was also pregnant. The following spring brought the birth of a third daughter, named Odel (the same Yiddish name as Hodel, Tevye's second daughter from *Fiddler On The Roof*), meaning 'thanks to the Almighty'. She may have lost a husband, but she was thankful for the daughter which arrived safely. But a single mother, now with three daughters, could not have found things easy. It may have been because of the poverty in which they found themselves that Ester's middle daughter Laje fell ill and passed away at the age of two on 30th April that same year, when little Odel was less than eight weeks old. The single word on Laje's death certificate for cause of death is *Abzehrung* – emaciation.

No records appear to exist telling us what might have happened to Ester and her two surviving daughters over the next twelve years – suggesting that she did not remarry. In need of an income, it may have been that she took over her husband's business as a baker, although the demands of motherhood might have made that impossible. Her eldest daughter Reizel may have been helping to run the house. What we do know is that in July 1844, Reizel was on the move out of Kempen. But she wasn't moving westward. At the age of eighteen, she was crossing the border into Poland to get married.

Natan Kohn was a merchant, born around the turn of the century around the same time as Ester. He lived in Kalisz with his wife and eight children; six sons and two daughters. The Kohns appear to have been a happy and healthy family, until tragedy struck in February 1844 when Natan's wife Lotte died. Her maiden name had been Lotte Gutmann. It's unclear whether Lotte and Ester were related, but certainly possible.

Judging from Natan's surname, it's highly likely that he was a *Kohen* – a member of the priestly class in Judaism claiming descent from the High Priest Aaron, brother of Moses. A *Kohen* needed to be respectable; a *Kohen* needed to be upstanding; a *Kohen* needed to be married. The call went out for a replacement bride for the forty-five-year-old Natan, and the answer was the eighteen-year-old Reizel. They were married on 18th July 1844 – which is surprising as this places the wedding during the Nine Days, a period of mourning leading up to the Fast of *Tisha B'Av* when the destruction of the Temple is commemorated. One might conclude that this is evidence of the speed with which Natan remarried, or the muted joy of a ceremony held less than six months after Lotte's death.

Reizel now found herself running a household where at least two of her stepsons were older than her. Nevertheless, she set to her tasks, including the bearing of more children for Natan the merchant. The names of the children born from this second marriage suggest that despite the 27-year age difference, Reizel was not the quiet submissive child bride who let her husband make all the decisions. Their first child was a boy, and his name was clearly her choice rather than Natan's. The boy was named Aron, after the father that Reizel lost to cholera when she was only five years old. Another boy came next, and then a daughter named Laje after the sister who died emaciated when Reizel was six. Two more daughters followed, and by their tenth wedding anniversary in 1854 Reizel and Natan had five children together, in addition to the offspring of Natan's first marriage to Lotte.

Natan had also changed occupation. He was no longer a

merchant, but an *oberżysta* – an innkeeper. This may have kept him home more than when he was a merchant; in any case he was getting older and approaching sixty. Living in a town with a large Jewish community concentrated in the only part of Kalisz where Jewish settlement was permitted, Natan may well have closed his tavern for Passover, as beer and other fermented drinks are not allowed during the festival. But as Passover came to an end in 1855, Natan was unable to reopen his inn. The day after the end of Passover, he died. Reizel was widowed at the age of twenty-nine, possibly even younger than her mother Ester when she experienced a similar loss.

Just like her mother, Reizel disappears from the records once widowed. If she did remarry there is no record of it. I'd like to think that she took over running the inn, even if the official ownership fell to one of Natan's sons from his first marriage; still full of energy, bringing up her own children aged between two and eight, and not needing a husband to tell her to get back in the kitchen or away from the account books. I hope that she was still going strong as the world continued to change around the family. The Poles tried their luck again – and lost again – against their Russian overlords in 1863 in the January Uprising, and as a result the official language changed from Polish to Russian (Reizel, if she had no husband to tell her not to, may have even been one of the Jewish women from Kalisz who made a battle banner for the Polish insurgents fighting in the area, with the inscription *"To our valiant Polish brothers, from Polish-Jewish women of Kalisz"*). Her stepchildren were married off by the 1870s when the railway arrived in the city, which was 45% Jewish by 1875.

Reizel would have been just about to turn fifty, if she did survive to stand under the *chuppa* (canopy) at the wedding that took place in Kalisz on 2nd August 1875 (also during the Nine Days leading up to *Tisha B'Av*, just like Reizel's wedding to Natan). Her middle daughter Perel was marrying a 22-year-old barber, whose signature at the bottom is the only recognisable non-Cyrillic writing on their marriage record. That name, in clear and precise script, was Markus Herszlik Zolty. The young couple settled down and immediately started a family. Their first son was born nine months and one week after the wedding, named Benjamin after Markus Herszlik's father. The second son, born three years later, was named for Perel's father – Nathan.

But as the new Zolty family began to take shape, the situation for Jews in Kalisz was getting worse. Thursday 20th June 1878 was the Feast Day of Corpus Christi, the Catholic celebration of the Eucharist. Like every year, the Feast was marked with a procession of altars and sacred imagery through the city – but this year, it was alleged that some of the altars had been vandalised in an attempt to sabotage the procession, and the supposed perpetrators were Jews. A mob broke off from the main procession and rampaged through the Jewish Quarter, destroying the synagogue as well as a number of homes and businesses. While the leaders of the mob were imprisoned after a subsequent investigation proved the allegations against the Jews to be false, the atmosphere in Kalisz was definitely poisoned.

Perel's family background gave the family an obvious choice for where to go next, to escape the worsening situation in Kalisz. At some point in the summer of 1880, the Zoltys crossed the border from Russian Poland into the relative safety of the German Empire. They headed for the nearest significant settlement across the border on the German railway line that had only been opened five years earlier. That line ran from Posen in the north to Kluczbork in the south – but most importantly it stopped at Kempen, the destination to which they were headed. Although it seems that they didn't go directly to Kempen straight away. They made enough of a stop at that first settlement for Perel to give birth to the child she was already carrying when they packed up and left Kalisz. No official record exists of the birth, but a census entry filled in much later in a different country tells us that Markus Herszlik and Perel's first daughter was born in Ostrawa in August 1880. That daughter was Rebecca Zolty, later known as Becky. My Polish Great-Grandma was born in Germany.

Following Becky's birth, the family completed their journey to Kempen. Two full birth records survive from their time there, but no flowing Cyrillic is to be seen – instead, the handwritten details are added in German between ruthlessly efficient typed Gothic lettering, as if it needed to be made any clearer that the family were now under the administration of the Second Reich. The names of the family members also reflect the change of location; Perel now appears as Paulina, while Markus Herszlik has become Hermann. The two daughters registered in Kempen were given names which could hardly have been further away from the Yiddish of the Polish *shtetl* – Helene and Salomea.

Germany was not as oppressive as Russian-occupied Poland (where things had only got worse after the assassination of Tsar Alexander II in 1881), but in the eyes of the Kempen community there were better places to live – chief among them still being the liberal, tolerant paradise around the mythical streets of Commercial Road and Petticoat Lane, dreamed about by Kempeners decades earlier when Perel's mother Reizel was growing up there. Hermann and Paulina (as Perel now was) suffered the pain of a stillbirth in 1885, and this may have been the event which triggered their exodus to London. Taking advantage of the new railways, they probably crossed Germany to Bremen or Hamburg on the North Sea coast, before taking ship for the Port of London. Becky was five years old.

The morning of Monday 1st March 1886 was the start of a new day, a new week, a new month and a new life for Becky and her two older brothers. The three of them were enrolled at the Jews' Free School in Bell Lane, Whitechapel, with probably only a few words of English between them. Their father's name (still Hermann), address (141 Wentworth Street) and dates of birth were carefully recorded in the same handwriting as every other pupil – that of JFS Headmaster Moses Angel, who had recorded the admission of Marks Markovitch to the school less than a year earlier. Becky would have received a very different education from her brothers; less maths and history, and more needlework and domestic accounting. Nevertheless, she learned not just to speak English but to read and write it too, with her progress through the levels recorded on the school roll. While the children were at school learning how to be English, Hermann found that his barbering skills were in demand among the densely packed population of the East End, and he set up in business as a hairdresser.

By 1891, Benjamin the eldest brother had left school and was working for his father in the family hairdressing salon. Things were going well; the census of that year shows the family still living in Wentworth Street, but in a bigger house which they did not share with any other families. The only non-Zolty living in their house was Sara Preseizen, a General Servant born in Poland. Pauline (the German 'a' at the end of her name had now become an English 'e') was able to afford some help with her seven children. The census return provides further proof of their Anglicisation – Helene was now Sophie, Salomea was now Sarah, and the two children born in England were Annie and Hettie. Sophie and Sarah had joined Becky at JFS, and Pauline might have considered how fortunate she was. Both her mother Reizel and her grandmother Ester had been widowed to bring up young families alone, while she had a husband and a domestic servant.

While Pauline escaped the fate of her mother and grandmother, her good fortune did not last much longer. On 14th April 1892, on the first of the *Chol Hamoed* days of Passover when normal activities are allowed, she died and was buried in West Ham Cemetery. Becky, now the oldest female in the family, was not yet twelve years old. She was still at school when her father remarried in 1893. Hermann was a member of the United Kalischer Synagogue in the East End, where the traditions and tunes of his home town were kept alive by *Kalischer Landsmen*. Six months after his second marriage, he was honoured by that shul through being named as that year's *Chatan Bereishit* – called up to *leyn* (chant) the very first verses of Genesis on the festival of *Simchas Torah* as the yearly cycle of reading the whole Five Books of Moses was ended and immediately restarted. The recognition of one's *shul* community, and the publishing of one's name in the Jewish Chronicle alongside the honourees from other synagogues, is as potent today as it was in the 1890s.

A photograph of Hermann and Pauline's children has

miraculously survived from around that time, perhaps commissioned by their father to mark the occasion judging from the ages which they appear to be. The seven children range in age from eighteen down to six; Benjamin the eldest is seated in a relaxed but serious pose, as befitting a young man already in the world of work. Annie, the youngest, is front and centre with a doll in her arms to keep her well-behaved. On the right, Nathan is looking after young Hetty, while standing at the back are the three sisters born in Germany; from left to right, Sarah with a slight smile, Sophie looking mildly terrified, and then Becky. I recognised Becky immediately as soon as I first saw the photograph, as she is unmistakeably the image of my Nanna (her daughter). Her head is slightly tilted to one side, and she appears pensive. As the oldest daughter, with a stepmother already pregnant with the start of a new family to demand her father's attention, she may have been feeling a weight of responsibility. She had just left school, and was only fourteen.

Hermann's new family was well underway by December 1895, when his Certificate of Naturalisation was issued. He was no longer an Alien but a British Subject, having sworn to be faithful and bear true allegiance to Her Majesty Queen Victoria and her Heirs and Successors. The certificate lists his nine children in order, from Benjamin down to 18-month-old Golda and 6-week-old Barnett, his children by his second wife. All these children now inherited Hermann's nationality. For the three boys, this was to have implications two decades later, when the First World War saw all of them in uniform for the British rather than the Russian Empire.

As the Victorian age came to a close and the new century started, the family continued to grow with three more daughters born to Hermann and his wife Rose in the space of four years: Jenny, Fanny and Miriam. The old Queen died, and the Zoltys had moved south of the River Thames to live in Southwark where Hermann was now a hairdresser and shopkeeper. Perhaps Becky was able to feel a little less responsible for everyone else and start planning her own future, but tragedy struck the family again. In 1903 her stepmother Rose passed away, still in her thirties. A second photograph to have survived down the generations shows Hermann with his second family; trying to guess the ages of the children, it seems impossible to determine whether this was taken shortly before or shortly after their mother's untimely death. Barnett, the only boy among the five children, cannot quite suppress the embarrassed grin that would be inevitable from any eight-year-old boy in such a situation, while the four girls surround their father, all looking straight at the camera with deadpan expressions.

Becky was once again the mother figure in the family, but there were two other sisters old enough to help her – and now that she was in her early twenties, her thoughts (or perhaps the expectations of those around her) turned to marriage. A decade or more earlier at JFS, she wouldn't have had much contact in lessons with the boys, but at the beginning and end of the school day boys and girls mixed freely in the *balagan* (chaos) outside the school gates. Family legend tells us that she got to know a lad who had started at the school less than year before she had, and who lived just a few streets away. By the end of 1905, 28-year-old Marks Markovitch was bringing in a regular wage as a boot maker. The impact of his JFS education was starting to wane through lack of practice; later in life he could still read but never really bothered with writing too much, signing his name with a simple cross. But he was handsome with a well-groomed Edwardian moustache, and he adored Becky as much then as he continued to do over the decades of their marriage. The childhood sweethearts got engaged, and plans were made for a wedding in the spring of 1906.

The marriage was celebrated at the Great Garden Synagogue in Whitechapel on 6th May 1906, but the mood of the event was not entirely one of celebration; Becky's expression in the official wedding photograph is one of steely determination rather than that of a blushing bride. Her father Hermann was very ill, and he died just twelve days after the wedding. His will contained a single bequest, to his daughter Sarah, of only twenty pounds; perhaps his illness had put the family in ever tighter financial circumstances. Three of the children from Hermann's second marriage – Barnett, Jane and Fanny

– were now underage orphans, subject to the administrative processes of the various Poor Law Unions for the areas in which the family had lived (a separate chapter could be written about Miriam the youngest, who escaped the orphanages by living with her half-sister Sarah and her new husband Harold Goldcrown; when Sarah died several decades later, she married Harold). The children were living in Hackney when their father died, but the Hackney Guardians saw them as Southwark's problem, since they had lived there for longer. It took until December for an solution to be agreed; at the expense of the Southwark Poor Law Union, the children would be allowed to stay where they were – at the Jews' Hospital and Orphan Asylum in Norwood. By then, Becky (who would no doubt have been making regular trips from her married home in Hackney to see her half-siblings in Norwood) was pregnant with her first child. On 30th April 1907, Pauline Markovitch – my Nanna – was born.

The strong Jewish matriarch is a well-worn cliché, but not without basis in fact. As I uncovered the story of my maternal female line, from Ester through Reizel, Perel and Becky to my Nanna Pauline and of course my mum, I discovered not just a succession of candle-lighting, *challah*-baking wives and mothers, but a great deal more. Like in the biblical Book of Ruth, what the men mostly do in this story is die – and leave the women to look after themselves and each other. Mum often tells me that my Nanna was in charge of the purse strings when she was growing up – Poppa Sidney may have been the breadwinner, but every penny passed under Nanna's control and every financial decision had her stamp on it. The same was almost certainly true of Becky, a generation earlier; with a husband who was uncomfortable writing his name, Becky would have been the one doing the accounts and handling communication with the outside world.

So it must have been even further back, either side of the border between Prussia and Poland. Ester and Reizel, both widowed early, picked up the responsibilities of providing for their young families and bringing them up safely. That look of steely determination in the eyes of my not-as-Polish-as-I-thought great-grandma comes from a long line of women who took what life threw at them and made the best of it, with or without men alongside them.

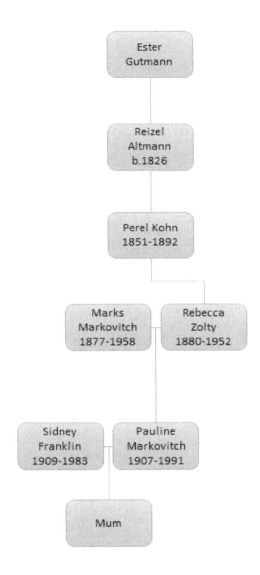

The border between the German and Russian Empires in 1880, where the Zoltys crossed from Kalisz to Ostrowo on the new railway line – the town where my great-grandmother Becky was born (Source: David Rumsey Map Collection, David Rumsey Map Center, Stanford Libraries)

The children of Hermann Zolty and Perel Kon, circa 1894. Back row: Sarah, Sophie, Becky. Front row: Benjamin, Ann, Nathan, Hettie

Hermann Zolty and his children from his second marriage (around 1902). Children L to R: Minnie, Fanny, Jenny, Golda, Barnett

"REJOICING OF THE LAW."

The following are the התני חתרה ובראשית at the undermentioned Synagogues :—

	חתן תורה	חתן בראשית
Bevis Marks,	Mr. Isaac Mendes	Mr. Jacob Mendes.
Bryanston Street,	Mr. Abraham I. Massias	Mr. Abraham Nahon.
Great,	Mr. M. Morris	Mr. Lewis Levy.
New,	Mr. Wolf Cohen	Mr. Isaac Rosalky.
Hambro,	Mr. David Joseph	Mr. J. Silverman.
St. John's Wood	Mr. Albert E. Moss	Mr. D. Lang.
Borough	Mr. W. H. Cohen	Mr. A. E. Hyman.
Hampstead	Mr. M. Diman	Mr. M. Eilenberg.
North London,	Mr. Hyam Barnett.	Mr. Eugene Woolstone
Dalston	Mr. N. Carper	Mr L. Schaap.
East London,	Mr. H. Chissick	Mr. A. Kirchenstein.
Hammersmith	Mr. B. J. Montague	Mr. Adolf Jacobs.
Western,	Mr. A. L. Sax	Mr. M. Simpson.
Maiden Lane,	Mr. J. L. Schier	Mr. H. Lewis.
South East London,	Mr. S. Bernstein	Mr. G. Koppenhagen.
Mildmay Park,	Mr. S. Coos	Mr. B. Wolf.
New Dalston	Mr. R. Benjamin	Mr. H. Benjamin.
Sandy's Row,	Mr. B. Vinkenstein	Mr. J. Rosenberg.
Spital Square	Mr. H. Fox	Mr. L. Jacobs.
Princes Street,	Mr. J Finkelstein	Mr. P. Barnett.
Old Castle Street,	Mr. J. Alexander	Mr. S. D. Beards.
New Road	Mr. W. Weber	Mr. I. Silverberg.
Poplar	Mr. B. Kempner	Mr. B. Cassell.
Maccabi Street	Mr. E. Lazarus	Mr. S. Davis.
United Kalischer,	Mr. J. Berg	Mr. H. Zolty.
Fashion Street,	Mr. S. Moses	Mr. H. Cash.
Plotzker	Mr. N. Saunders	Mr. M. Goldberg.

Simchat Torah honourees at various synagogues, 29th September 1893, listing Hermann Zolty as Chatan Bereishit at the United Kalischer Synagogue (image courtesy of the Jewish Chronicle)

Becky Markovitch nee Zolty - my 'Polish' Great-Grandma (1880-1952)

Childhood sweethearts? Becky Zolty & Marks Markovitch on their wedding day, 1906

7 The Lyons Corner House Link

It was early in my family history research journey that the surname 'Lyons' appeared in my mum's ancestry – the birth certificate of my great-great-grandfather Samuel Marks (born in a brothel, although I didn't know that at the time) named his mother as Hannah Marks née Lyons. Straight away, Mum was convinced that this was a link to *the* Lyons family – she was sure that she remembered her dad (my Poppa, whose relationship with the truth was always pleasingly flexible) saying that we were in some way linked to the family behind J. Lyons & Co and the famous Lyons Corner Houses of the early and mid-twentieth century.

The man who gave his name to the Lyons restaurant chain and related brands was Joseph Lyons (1847-1917). His mother was a Hannah Lyons (after her marriage – her maiden name was Cohen) and he was the son of a watch and jewellery seller. When he went into partnership with brothers Isidore and Montague Gluckstein to enter the catering business, it was the Lyons name that the three of them agreed to use as the name of the company. When I first read that, I thought – well that makes sense; in the 1880s, the name Gluckstein would have been perhaps a little too 'exotic' to have the mass appeal that was needed. (Sad to say, that may still be true in the twenty-first century.) In fact, the truth was quite different. The Gluckstein brothers thought that associating their name with catering would be beneath them, so Lyons was the name they used. Were it not for the snobbery of Isidore and Montague, twentieth century London could have had 250 Gluckstein Teashops serving the capital's population with tea, scones and light suppers. Although I'm not sure if Lyons Maid ice cream would have been quite as successful if it was Gluckstein Maid.

All of which is tangential at best to my family history, as I was unable to find any link between Joseph Lyons and my great-great-great-grandmother Hannah. Joseph's grandfather was born in Germany in 1784 and lived in South London, while Hannah's family were very much based north of the river in Houndsditch. Lyons (or Lyon – families seemed to be relaxed between using either spelling of the name) was a common Jewish surname across Europe in the early nineteenth century, related to the Hebrew names *Leib* or *Arye* ('Lion' in Yiddish and Hebrew respectively). What I found out about the Lyon family with whom I *can* prove a link was perhaps even more remarkable than tea shops.

Hannah Marks née Lyons died on 28th July 1868 in Hackney. Her days of running a West End 'lodging house' were well behind her; most of her children were married and living further out from Whitechapel and Central London, where Hannah had lived most of her life. The family were now spread across Mile End, Hackney and Islington. With her as she passed away was her eldest daughter Sarah, who also witnessed the execution of the will a few months later together with Hannah's eldest son Lewis. But news of her death went a great deal further; in the fledgling Colony of Victoria on the other side of the world, the Melbourne Argus reported it in this way:

On the 28th of July, at 63 Hackney-road, London. Hannah, relict of the late Elias Marks, the beloved mother of Mrs. David Cohen, and sister of Mr. David Lyons of this city, aged sixty-two, sincerely regretted by all who knew her.

Mrs. David Cohen was Hannah and Elias's daughter Rachael Marks, born in 1833 and married to David Cohen in Victoria in 1857. As for Hannah's brother David "of this city", this was a new character whom I hadn't yet come across, although it wasn't difficult to find out more about him. David Lyons was a big player in

Melbourne in the second half of the nineteenth century – a wealthy magnate with a mansion on the edge of the city in the fashionable suburb of St. Kilda. The *Chronicles of Early Melbourne* relate how he started the first candle-making establishment in the city, before taking office as the third Sheriff's officer that Melbourne ever had. David, the *Chronicles* tell us, "*…succeeded with everything he took in hand. He was one of the most enterprising of the old colonists; and at Sydenham, on the Brighton Road, in the sunset of life, reaped the reward of a long career of honourable industry until his death.*" In 1867, when His Royal Highness Prince Albert, Duke of Edinburgh visited Melbourne, the Address of Loyalty to the Prince – signed by the prominent figures of the city – included David's signature. On his death in 1883, he was buried in the vault dug especially for him in the Church of England portion of the Melbourne General Cemetery; an area of twelve feet by sixteen feet topped by a massive stone block engraved with David's name. This was a substantial and respected gentleman.

David's will, preserved in the archives of the State of Victoria and running to six pages of detailed bequests and instructions, is a treasure trove of detail into the family back in London with whom he was clearly still in contact right up to his death. The legacies paid to relatives in England alone amounted to more than a thousand pounds – over £100,000 in today's money. Hannah gets a mention on page one, in the first bequests after those to David's wife Amelia; "*to my nieces Maria Myers, Julia Myers and Sarah Moses all of London in England the daughters of my deceased sister Hannah.*" All three of these nieces were born to Hannah and Elias in the West End and were now married. David also mentions other relatives – all females; although David had a significant number of nephews back in England, none of them received a penny. Every bequest was to a niece or a still-living sister. In one case, David mentioned a half-sister; Rosa Isaacs received a whopping two hundred and fifty pounds from David's will (the will also mentions that David was already "*in the habit of*" sending her thirteen pounds twice a year, which he insisted should still be sent until the full legacy was paid). This half-sister would later prove to be a key clue to finding out more about David and Hannah's origins.

Discovering this Australian magnate put me in touch with a cousin I never knew I had — a direct descendant of his, who still carries the Lyons surname. Joining forces, with his knowledge of the Lyons family history in Melbourne and my research into the London side of the family, we managed to solve the mystery of how David got to Australia. My Antipodean cousin, raised on stories of David the wealthy entrepreneur, took some convincing to accept his ancestor's backstory. But as for me, already knowing some of Hannah's activities, I wasn't the least bit surprised.

Tuesday 6th October 1829 started the same as any other day for Thomas Saunders, a watchmaker with a shop on Whitechapel Road. He unlocked the door of his shop at about seven o'clock, and stood in the parlour readying himself for whatever business the day might bring. When he sensed that a young man was in the shop itself which fronted the street, he assumed that it was his son; but as he walked in, the young man removed his hands from where they had been in one of Thomas's glass cases, and ran out of the open front door. As the young man stumbled out into the street, he dropped a number of metal objects. Ignoring them, he continued his attempted escape into the busy London morning. Thomas looked at the glass case, and saw that one of the trays in that case was missing six penknives.

A few moments later, two people entered the shop. Anthony Thompson, a local resident, was holding eighteen-year-old David by the scruff of his neck, having grabbed him as he ran down the road. Another local picked up the knives from where they had fallen by the door and returned them to Thomas. Protesting his innocence, David was taken to the watch-house with Thomas following on to press charges. An argument between the watch-maker and the teenager couldn't be resolved there, so the case went to court. Three weeks later, David was on trial at the Old Bailey. His defence was simple — it wasn't him that took (and then dropped) the knives, and he happened to be running down the road at the time on an urgent errand for his master. Thomas Saunders was now convinced that David was the youngster he saw in his shop that morning.

For the sake of six penknives worth just a shilling each, David Lyons was sentenced to be transported to Tasmania for seven years. He was moved to Portsmouth where he spent eleven months on prison ships at anchor just off the coast – miserable, crowded hulks that served as holding pens for prisoners until a ship was ready to take them across the oceans. That ship was the *John*, which David joined on the third of its six voyages to Australia between 1827 and 1836. He arrived in Van Diemen's Land in January 1831. His convict record is a mix of occasional misadventures (mostly involving overindulgence in alcohol after hours) and a number of assignments which suggest that he was quite valuable to the penal colony. David learned many of the skills that would help him starting out to make his fortune later in life; candle-making, brick-making and accounting. On 12th April 1839, having served his sentence, he stepped off a very different ship – the *Adelaide* – onto shore at Port Phillip as a free man. He was only twenty-eight.

Port Phillip was the harbour district of what was just starting to become the settlement of Melbourne. David was there pretty much at the very start of the city's story, along with a number of other newly freed colonists who became the movers and shakers of the new colony of Victoria. In April 1840 he married Amelia Oliver, an assisted passenger just off the boat from England in one of the many ships filled with single women bringing 'marrying material' to the male dominated colonies. The ceremony took place in the Parish Church of St. James Melbourne, officiated by the Reverend James Wilson. David and Amelia's numerous children were all baptised, as one would expect of an upwardly mobile Victorian gentleman eager to present himself as the model of a mainstream, respectable Christian.

But some those children's names tell a different story – Samuel, Rachel and Hannah (three of his first five children) could very easily have been names he took with him from his Jewish childhood in London. My new Australian cousin told me that his grandfather and great-grandfather (respectively a grandson and son of David) both described themselves as Jewish, if only by descent rather than practice. While he may not have told the world about his controversial past, both criminal and Hebraic, he certainly didn't forget it.

Which brings us to the search for David and Hannah's parents. Their father's name proved something of a mystery; David's death certificate in 1883 names his father as Lyon Lyons, but Hannah and three other brothers all named their eldest sons Lewis – another common English equivalent of the Hebrew name *Yehuda Leib* which appears on Hannah's marriage record. The half-sister mentioned in David's will can be identified as Rosetta Davis, born in 1821. So (and I hope you're all following this), it seems that Hannah and David's mother was married twice – first to their Lyons father, and then to a Henry Davis who was Rosetta's father. (Interestingly, Rosetta Davis married Coleman Isaacs in 1839 to become the "Rosa Isaacs" mentioned in David's will. This is not the first time that Coleman gets a mention in this book; back in Chapter 2 he was the witness to the death of Elias Marks, brothel owner and Coleman's wife's half-sister's husband.) So, if I could find a Lewis (or Lyon) Lyon (or Lyons) who died in Whitechapel or thereabouts between David's birth in 1813 and Rosetta's birth in 1821, I could be pretty sure that this was the right man.

Reader, I found him.

The Sun Fire Insurance Policy Registers held in the London Metropolitan Archives record that on 4th February 1815, while Napoleon was on Elba plotting his return to France, the widow Mary Lyon took over the insurance policy on 9 Shoemakers Row, Aldgate following the death of tailor and woollen draper Lewis Lyon. Lewis had left other evidence of his existence; the original insurance policy, as well as tax records from Cree Church Lane in Houndsditch. On Boxing Day 1796 the 23-year-old 'taylor' was initiated into Hiram's Lodge in the Minories, one of the earliest Jewish Freemasons' Lodges in England. The evidence is clear that Lewis paid his taxes, did his job and obeyed the law.

Others, however, were less diligent in keeping to their obligations and paying their debts. Lewis is mentioned in the *London Gazette* of 7th May 1814 as a creditor of Levy Levy, a bankrupt in debtor's prison. Levy Levy also appears in a remarkable document dated 17th February 1815, just a short time after Lewis's death; not his will, but *"A Declaration instead of a true, perfect and particular inventory of all and singular the Goods Chattels and Credits of Lewis Lyon in the County of Middlesex Taylor deceased, made and rendered by virtue of the Corporal Oath of Mary Lyon Widow"*. The handwritten pages of this Declaration describe every item Lewis possessed (valued in total at one hundred and fifty pounds), and goes on to list all the sums of money which, according to Mary, were due to him before his demise. Mary lists twenty-one bills or promissory notes – IOUs, in the language of my generation – amounting to a staggering £560 (and 15 shillings) that Lewis had the paperwork to collect on. That wasn't even the end of the list; the IOUs are followed by forty-six named individuals who owed money *"for Goods sold and delivered"*, totaling a further £344, three shillings and ninepence. The names of Lewis's debtors are almost all recognisably Jewish – Isaacs, Myers, Levy, Lipman, Solomon, Israel, Harris and Jacobs are only a few of the full list. Dozens of Jews all over Whitechapel owed money to the tailor, whom we can only assume to have been very bad indeed at calling in debts.

The most striking evidence for Lewis's lack of judgement around money is a surviving scroll of parchment which unrolls to a single sheet more than a metre tall and a metre across, inscribed with approximately four thousand words (I haven't counted, just estimated) of almost impenetrable nineteenth century legalese. Dated 12th November 1813, it is addressed to the Lord High Chancellor, the head of the judiciary and presiding officer of the House of Lords. The document, even more troublesome to read than it is to handle, tells the story of how poor Lewis came to be in a position where legal action was being taken against him by two individuals who claimed that Lewis was liable, thanks to a complex web of contracts and indentures, for large sums of money. Lewis was a humble tailor, living at that time in Cree Church Lane in Houndsditch, whereas the two individuals coming after him were Samuel Birch and William

Heygate, both of whom were to be separately elected Lord Mayor of London over the next few years. It was not a contest of equals.

It seems that when Birch and Heygate were appointed to be Sheriffs of the City of London, they appointed a certain William Clipson as one of their officers. Delegating responsibility to a Sheriff's Officer was not without risk, so Birch and Heygate required Clipson to commit to being liable to large amounts of money should he fail to carry out his duties and put the Sheriffs at risk of prosecution themselves. Clipson needed help to be able to guarantee that he could meet such a liability, so he gathered a group of six Londoners to stand as sureties for him – an oysterman, a vintner, a flour factor, a baker, a brandy merchant and of course a tailor in the form of Lewis himself. In 1811 Birch and Heygate assumed office as Sheriffs, and the agreement between them, Clipson and the six guarantors was written up and signed. Lewis was becoming connected to the people who ran the City through its guilds and corporations; one imagines him coming home to his wife Mary and his young family (including the four-year-old Hannah) proud of how he was laying the foundations for the social advancement of the Lyon family. It all rested on William Clipson acting as a responsible, honest and diligent Sheriff's Officer.

Lewis's humble petition describes what happened once Clipson took office: *"in the course of that time the said William Clipson did various acts as such officer which were contrary to his duty, and by means and in consequence thereof the said Samuel Birch and William Heygate… became liable to pay and were obliged to pay certain sums of money to a large amount."*

In short, Clipson was a crook. In April 1812, Lewis was informed that as one of the six sureties, he was liable for £390 to make up for Clipson's corruption in office. So much for his entry into the higher echelons of London society. The six guarantors managed to get Clipson to sell his house with the intention of using the proceeds to satisfy the Sheriffs. It looked like the matter was closed – until Lewis suddenly found that legal action was being taken against him, and only him. The petition tells how the other five guarantors, in league with Clipson, Birch, Heygate and others, went to court claiming that

Lewis still owed money in connection with the original surety. Lewis was now looking at a legal demand for one hundred and sixty-four pounds, nineteen shillings and sixpence, with two of the most powerful men in London chasing him for the money. With no other recourse, he must have decided to take his case straight to the top; his petition was drawn up and sent to the Lord Chancellor.

The outcome of Lewis's petition is unknown, but I think it unlikely that the result was a favourable one. Samuel Birch and William Heygate both continued to rise to become not only Lord Mayors of London but, in Heygate's case, an MP and ultimately Baronet of Southend. William Clipson appears again, perhaps not surprisingly, as one of Lewis's debtors in the list compiled by Mary after his death. As for the other five guarantors, one has to wonder why they all seem to have turned on the Jewish member of their group (there may have been other Jewish guarantors besides Lewis, but the names suggest otherwise) – was he perhaps the easy target to take the fall for the rest of them? It remains an open question whether Lewis's untimely death in 1815 was in any way hastened by the humiliation, stress and trauma to which this whole case must have subjected him.

As a final postscript to this episode, I take some comfort from the way that Samuel Birch and William Heygate have been remembered. Typing their names into Google Images returns only two images which feature them both together. One is a rather dull monochrome print of the two of them being presented to the Court of Exchequer in 1811. The second is a brightly coloured satirical cartoon from 1820, showing seven Lord Mayors of London protesting ineffectually against prayers being said for Queen Caroline, George IV's consort famously hated by the establishment and loved by the people. Birch and Heygate are both named, and appear as donkey-eared, wine-soaked 'false prophets', clearly the butt of the cartoonist's joke. That's certainly how I choose to see them.

It doesn't look like Lewis's widow Mary had much luck calling in the debts which were owed to him. In 1817 she was on the witness stand at the Old Bailey – and so was her daughter Hannah, at only ten years of age. In a deliberate attempt to make things difficult for family history researchers two centuries later, the trial featured two Mary Lyonses: Mary Lyons the witness, and Mary Lyons the defendant. They were related – Hannah describes Mary the witness as her mother, and Mary the defendant as her aunt. It appears that there were two Lyons brothers who both took wives with the same given name.

A weaver in Bethnal Green had been burgled in February with a selection of material and clothing taken, including 24 yards of satin worth five pounds. The satin was next seen a few days later, when a man calling himself 'Franks' deposited it at a pawnbroker in the Minories (one of the main streets separating the City of London and Whitechapel). The next part of the story was related to the Court by ten-year-old Hannah, for whom the experience of giving testimony can only have been terrifying, exciting or perhaps both:

"I gave the ticket to my mother. I received it from the prisoner. She said my uncle wanted to sell it. She is my aunt."

The pawnbroker's ticket was passed from Mary the defendant, via young Hannah, to Mary Hannah's mother. It was Hannah's mother who used the ticket to get the satin from the pawn shop. While Mary the defendant was unable to explain how she came to be in possession of the pawn shop ticket, there was no evidence that she was the burglar. A verdict of not guilty was returned, and we can assume that Hannah, her mother and her aunt returned home unscarred from this brush with the law.

But who was the mysterious uncle who wanted to sell the satin cloth? He must have been a brother of the deceased Lewis, who was perhaps looking after his brother's family following Lewis's death. Hannah was ten, but David (the future convict, entrepreneur and Australian magnate) was just four years old at the time of his aunt's trial. This uncle – the would-be seller of stolen cloth – was perhaps the first father figure that David would have known.

As we exchanged emails and insights, my distant cousin and I came to the conclusion that we could identify this uncle. I have already mentioned that David's death certificate in 1883 names his father as Lyon Lyons; we think that his family assumed that this was his natural father, when in fact it was his uncle. And if Hannah and David did have an uncle who was keen on selling stolen goods, there is a wealth of evidence for a Lyon Lyons, from Cree Church Lane in Houndsditch (the same address as on Lewis's 1813 petition), who fitted that exact description.

The *Globe* newspaper reported on Monday 2nd July 1827 from Mansion House (the residence and place of work of the Lord Mayor of London) that *"the office was crowded this morning in consequence of Lyon Lyons, of Houndsditch, another notorious Jew 'Fence' coming up for examination on a charge of having stolen property in his possession."* This was the first of a number of times that Lyon was questioned, with reporters eager to tell the reading public how his long career of handling of stolen goods had finally landed him in court on two separate charges of theft, only a day apart from each other. Two weeks later, the Hampshire Advertiser carried a report of his final questioning before trial at the Old Bailey:

"On Saturday, the front of the Mansion-house was at an early hour completely besieged by hundreds of the most notorious Jew thieves and receivers of stolen goods that the metropolis can boast of, the inhabitants of the back slums of Houndsditch, Petticoat-lane, and the whole of the neighbourhood being congregated together, anxious to know the fate of one HENRY SOLOMONS, father of the notorious Ikey Solomons, who had been apprehended on the preceding day by Mr. Cope the Marshal on a charge of felony; and also of LYON LYONS, a most extensive receiver and partner of Ikey, who had been before examined, and whose final examination was fixed for Saturday."

More about Lyon's partner, the notorious Ikey Solomons, later. So began six years of trials, appeals, pleas and petitions which suggest that there was no excuse or justification, however outlandish, which Lyon and his wife would not employ in the service of trying to avoid punishment.

His first trial, on 12th July 1827 at the Old Bailey, was on a charge of stealing a selection of cut glass 'smelling bottles' from a chemist in Piccadilly. The bottles in question were found in Lyon's house and were proved to be the same as those that went missing. Lyon was in trouble. Fortunately, he was able to call on three friends good and true – Philip Phillips, Joel David and Joseph Emmanuel – to provide his much-needed alibi. They testified that Lyon was with them at the theatre on 23rd June. On hearing this, one can imagine that the prosecutor must have been wearing a smile and barely suppressing a giggle as he got up to address the judge: *"My Lord, this robbery was on the 16th."*

Philip Phillips, who was perhaps experienced at defending the indefensible, barely missed a beat and switched to a distinct memory of Lyon being ill on the 16th. Joseph Hart backed him up and further added that Lyon was taken ill the day before, so he couldn't have left the house on the day of the robbery. Lyon's own defence was short and to the point: *"I am nearly sixty years old, and have been ill for twelve months, and was never in prison, as to the bottles, I leave that entirely to my Counsel."*

The jury didn't buy the sick old man routine and found him guilty. No sentence was passed - judgement was respited until Lyon could be tried for the second charge two months later. This time the stolen goods were worth a lot more; 12 yards of wool, 96 pairs of white kid gloves, and bills of exchange amounting to over one thousand pounds – all removed from the premises of a wool manufacturer on Cheapside on 17th June 1827. Again, a significant proportion of the stolen items had been found in Lyon's house (not the bills of exchange – presumably these were turned into cash straight away) and these items were positively identified as being the exact items taken from the Cheapside premises. At his second trial, Lyon once again called on a number of 'friends' to attest to his character and to his poor health at the time of the robbery. Joseph Hart was back, still maintaining that Lyon was too ill to be any part of a smash-and-grab raid. Henry Harris, Lewis Lazarus, Mordecai Moses and Solomon Levy all described how they had known the accused for many years, and that he was an honest and scrupulous general dealer, always attending sales to buy and sell cloth, ribbons and muslins.

Lyon himself said only a few words at his second trial. He was very ill (he said), and should feel obliged if the Court would allow his written defence to be read out. This written defence – which would have taken about twenty minutes to read out in full – does not appear in the official Court transcript, but the *Morning Chronicle* of 14th September 1827 carries it word for word. It opened like this:

"My Lord, and Gentlemen of the Jury – I stand before you in some of the most extraordinary circumstances in the world, and at the same time in circumstances the most distressing to myself, innocent as I am... I must trespass a little on your patience..."

He goes on to ridicule the notion that he could break into a warehouse (*"Me! A sickly, infirm, aged man! Me!"*) He points to his clean record, and how unlikely it would be that he could be *"suddenly transformed, in my old age and leaded with infirmity, into a desperate robber... is it not utterly incredible?"* He then bamboozles the jurors with every possible reason why there might be doubt over his involvement in the crime. Yes, he had possessed the goods, but the law prohibits *recent* possession, and he was found with the stolen goods weeks after the robbery! As for evidence, he had brought reams of paperwork to this trial to prove that he was an honest dealer; admittedly, none of the paperwork actually related to the stolen goods in question – but *"buying and selling for ready money without the formality of bills and receipts... is much too common to be considered an infallible test of criminality."* Finally, Lyon repeats that he was ill and bedridden at home on the night in question, and declares that *"I shall leave myself in the hands of the Court, confident that no impartial tribunal can deem me the desperate offender who committed the robbery for which I am now upon my trial."*

As an Ashkenazi Jew, Lyon would have probably been familiar with the Yiddish word *chutzpah*. He certainly possessed it in significant quantities. The jury, however, weren't convinced. He was found guilty again, and this time the judge was able to pass sentence. Lyon was taken away to face seven years' transportation to Australia. Arriving in Portsmouth, he was assigned to the *HMS York*, a former Royal Navy ship of the line converted to a prison hulk.

It's not clear why, but Lyon never made it to Australia. He does appear in the lists of *HMS Hardy*, a small brig which served as a hospital to the other hulks – no doubt he took every opportunity to use his sickness and infirmity to get him away from any scenario where he might have set sail and lost any chance of getting home. While Lyon lingered (or possibly malingered) on the *Hardy*, efforts were made to get him released or his sentence commuted. A petition dated October 1829 was sent to Robert Peel, then Home Secretary and soon to be Prime Minister. The appeal for sympathy didn't hold back at all – Lyon was *"in Ill Health and a Disorder in the Eyes... with a Wife and a family of Four Girls, two of which are unfortunately Deaf and Dumb... reduced to the utmost Extremity of Poverty."*

It didn't seem to help; In 1829 Robert Peel had other things to worry about, setting up the Metropolitan Police in that very year and getting both his first name and surname into general usage as slang for policemen. Nevertheless, the appeals to Peel continued. In November 1829, nineteen residents of Houndsditch and the surrounding areas added their signatures to a plea for clemency on Lyon's behalf. In March 1830, a letter from an H. Reynolds tried to follow up on the petition sent some months earlier.

June 1830 saw a new king on the throne, and Lyon grabbed the chance to take his case to the very top. Carefully filed in the National Archives in Kew is Lyon's Humble Petition to *"His Most Gracious Majesty William the Fourth, King of Great Britain."* The back of the petition has a few lines to identify the convict to whom it relates, adding the line *"Character on board ship: Very Good. Blind & Infirm."* The petition itself revisited the points made in previous documents – his infirmity, his near-blindness, his unsupported wife and four daughters. He also had the *chutzpah* to describe himself to the King as *"upwards of Sixty Years of Age"*, less than three years after every document relating to his conviction gives his age as fifty-five. The final petition that can be found in the archives is not from Lyon but from his wife Mary in June 1832, directed at Peel's successor as Home Secretary, Viscount Melbourne. Lyon was now a patient on board a new hospital ship, the *HMS Alonzo.*

Whether it was thanks to Mary's petition or Lyon's declining health, in the following year he finally saw some clemency from the authorities. The 'How Discharged' column in his ship records, which for most prisoners gave the date of their departure for Australia, was finally updated with the entry *"PFP 29 July 33"*. Six years into his seven-year transportation sentence, without having been transported further than Gosport in Hampshire, Lyon Lyons was pardoned and released. It's likely that he returned to London, although his health may not have held out for long.

Which only leaves the unanswered question of Lyon's partner in receiving and handling stolen goods, the notorious Ikey Solomons. Ikey (a diminutive of Isaac) was something of a celebrity in the late 1820s following his dramatic escape from custody and subsequent adventures across Europe, America and Australia. Stories of his criminal activity, and the way he used gangs of young pickpockets to supply him with stolen goods, became commonplace among the literary circles of London. By 1836, one London writer was ready to use Ikey as the basis for a character in his next novel. That writer was Charles Dickens, and the novel was *Oliver Twist*. Lyon Lyons's partner Ikey Solomons was the original Fagin.

Having started out investigating this branch of the family looking for tea-room entrepreneurs, what I found was a pair of brothers; both living in Houndsditch in the early years of the nineteenth century, and both trying to make their way in the world using very different approaches. Lewis the honest tailor made every effort to make his mark in mainstream society, granting credit to dozens of his customers and trusting those with links to the City authorities, for all the good it did him in the end. And his brother Lyon? Well, perhaps he just found that he had to pick a pocket or two.

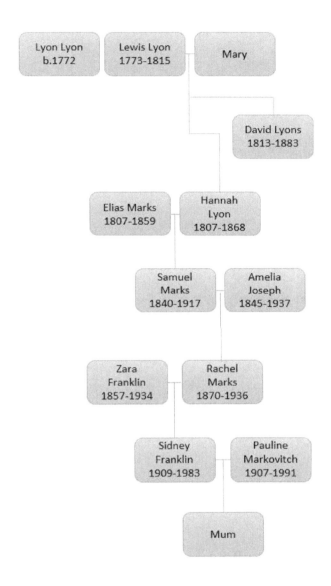

[In order to guard against imposition, notices o
Births, Marriages, and Deaths must be authenticated
by some respectable person in Melbourne to insure
their insertion.]

MARRIAGE.

JUNIPER—TYLER.—On the 28th ult., at Preston, by
the Rev. S. Day, of Geelong, William, youngest son
of John Juniper, Esq., Tylden, to Lydia, youngest
daughter of James Tyler, Esq., Preston. All formerly of Brighton, Sussex.

DEATHS.

ELLIOTT.—On the 1st June, from sunstroke, Charles
Sandys Elliott, Esq., H. M. Military Store Staff,
commissioner on special service to Abyssinia,
second son of the late James Elliott, Esq., solicitor,
of London and Geelong.

MARKS.—On the 28th of July, at 63 Hackney-road,
London, Hannah, relict of the late Elias Marks,
the beloved mother of Mrs. David Cohen, and sister
to Mr. David Lyons of this city, aged sixty-two,
sincerely regretted by all who knew her.

OSBORNE.—On the 22nd June, at Alvaston, near
Derby, England, James Osborne, Esq., uncle of Mr.
M. W. Osborne of this city.

*Hannah Marks née Lyons' death reported in the Melbourne Argus, October
1868 (Source: newspaperarchive.com)*

David Lyons' grave and family vault, Melbourne General Cemetery

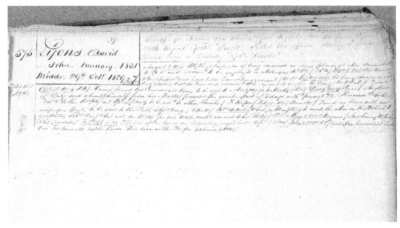

Description of David Lyons on his arrival in Van Diemen's Land, 1831.
Source: Tasmanian Archives CON18/1/9.

Conduct Record of David Lyons, 1829-1839. Source: Tasmanian Archives
CON31/1/28, no. 575.

The Petition of Lewis Lyons to the Lord High Chancellor, 1813 (Image courtesy of the National Archives, Kew)

MANSION - HOUSE. — IKEY SOLOMONS' FATHER.—On Saturday, the front of the Mansion-house was at an early hour completely besieged by hundreds of the most notorious Jew thieves and receivers of stolen goods that the metropolis can boast of, the inhabitants of the back slums of Houndsditch, Petticoat-lane, and the whole of the neighbourhood being congregated together, anxious to know the fate of one HENRY SOLOMONS, the father of the notorious *Ikey Solomons*, who had been apprehended on the preceding day by Mr. Cope, the Marshal, on a charge of felony; and also of LYON LYONS, a most extensive receiver, and partner of Ikey, who had been before examined, and whose final examination was fixed for Saturday.

A RECEIVER.—Lyon Lyons, described as a second Ikey Solomons, was tried at the Old Bailey, on Thursday, on a charge of stealing cloth, bills of exchange, gloves, and other property, value 1,515l., the property of Mr Matthew Waller, a warehouseman, in King-Street, Cheapside. Henry Hall deposed, that he is a clerk to the prosecutor, whose warehouse is at No. 19, in King-Street, Cheapside; on the night of the 16th June last, between six and seven in the evening, the premises were made secure; on the Monday morning, the 18th of June, about half-past eight o'clock, he arrived at the premises, and found they had been entered, and cloths, and other property to a large amount, had been carried off. The robbers had entered from Cateaton-Street; a pannel had been cut out of a door, and the door opened; two desks were broken open, a quantity of gloves and cigars, also three gold watches, bills of exchange, value about 1,000l., and about twenty bales of cloth, value 400l. were stolen. The robbers had drunk a bottle of wine, and smoked cigars on the premises. Mr Cope, City Marshal of London, said, that he went to the prisoner's house, in Cock and Hoop-Yard, Houndsditch, on the 28th of June, and found about ten yards of woollen cloth, and five dozen of French gloves; witness produced them; this property was sworn to be part of that stolen. The prisoner put in a written defence, urging the improbability, that infirm as he was, he should have permitted to associate with men, capable of committing the daring robbery described. Several witnesses bore testimony to his character, and described him as a general dealer. The jury, however, found him guilty.

Lyon Lyons in the Hampshire Advertiser, 16th July 1827.

Lyon Lyons' trial in the Newcastle Courant, 22nd Sept 1827.

8 The Revolutionary

"My Uncle Joe would have loved you two!" was the remark, sometimes accompanied by a weary sigh, that my brother and I would often hear whenever our dad was presented with evidence of the latest progressive political view that one or both of us were espousing. With parents who lived in suburban Middlesex, read the *Daily Mail* and voted Conservative through the Thatcher years, having a Communist in the family tree was definitely something out of the ordinary.

This was the Joe whose only child was Celia – the relative whom I interviewed at the very start of my research journey, around ten years before her death in 1999. The story that she told me was similar to that which appears, told by her, in the chronicles of the Ben Uri Art Society, of which her father was a founder member. Joe was my grandpa's half-brother, born in 1882 to Chaim Myer Przybysz, a poor butcher in Rawa Mazowiecka. Joe's mother Gitel died shortly afterwards, so Chaim Myer married his dead wife's younger sister Freda (my great-grandmother). Joe's ethical principles stopped him from joining his father in the slaughtering business, so he became a tailor. He joined various revolutionary societies, and was one of many young hotheads who were imprisoned by the Russian secret police for political activity in the 1905 revolution. Joe was about to be sent to the freezing wastes of Siberia when a general amnesty in 1906 allowed him a chance to leave. The Tsar's men advised him never to show his face in the Russian Empire again, so he travelled around Europe looking for a new home before arriving in London. It was there that he met a young actress named Dinah Krieger, and fell in love. They married in 1908, and Celia was born in 1913 – by which time Joe's half-brothers and half-sisters were starting to arrive in England. He then devoted the rest of his life to art, literature and politics through his leadership of the Ben Uri Society, his involvement in Yiddish language projects and the continuation of his left-wing activities through the decades before and after the Second World War. Such was the story that I had in mind when I began delving deeper into this fascinating character, trying to discover how much was true and how much was – well – less true.

The first unexpected thing which I learned about Uncle Joe went all the way back to his birth. Thanks to the internet and the Church of Jesus Christ of Latter-day Saints, his birth record was a document which I was able to locate and get a copy of, albeit in Russian. His birthdate was not the same as the one on later documents, but not different by much; later in life Joe claimed to have been born on 22nd May 1882, but according to the original record it was 11th June (by the Gregorian calendar; 30th May in the Julian calendar). The parents named on the birth record matched what we already knew – Chaim Myer Przybysz and Gitel Weinberg. The child's name was slightly different, as it was *Idel*, the Yiddish diminutive version of *Yudeleh*, which itself was a version of the Hebrew *Yehuda* (Judah). Over the course of his life, Uncle Joe went from *Idel* to *Yuda* to *Guda* to Judah to Joe, with the occasional Joseph thrown in for good measure.

There was one more thing on his birth record which surprised me. Immediately before his mother Gitel's name was the word *девица (devitsa)* – which, my online translation tools told me, means 'maiden'. And the word *жена (zhena* = wife) did not appear anywhere. Everyone I had spoken to about this side of the family was quite definite about Chaim Myer's two marriages to two sisters, but this suggested otherwise. Confirmation came when I managed to find and translate Gitel's death certificate. She died on 29th December 1885, at five o'clock in the morning. A note I made (without recording the source, sadly) relates that someone in the family had told me that she died 'after a fall'. At five in the morning in late December? One can only imagine that an early morning errand resulted in an icy slip which was tragically fatal. Little Idel, at three and a half years old, had lost his mother. Little Idel was also, it seems, born out of wedlock. That was something that was never mentioned in any of the conversations I had with older family members about Uncle Joe. He may not have even known it himself.

It's certainly possible that his Aunt Freda, Gitel's younger sister, was around a great deal to help look after the newly motherless Idel. Gitel had two other siblings – a brother who may have already left Poland by this date, and another sister who was only eleven. Freda was nineteen, and it was less than three months after Gitel's death that a wedding took place which must have been something of an unusual affair. If Chaim Myer and Gitel had been planning to marry, this would have been exactly the event that would have taken place – the same location, the same *khusen* (groom), the same groom's family and the same bride's family. Just the *kallah* (bride) was different, in a strange inversion of a Levirate marriage (when a widow marries her dead husband's brother).

Over the next decade and more, Idel's family steadily got bigger as Chaim Myer and Freda provided him with a succession of half-sisters and half-brothers (technically three-quarter-siblings rather than half-siblings, as Gitel and Freda were sisters – that's just in case any of this needs to be made more complicated). By 1904 he would have been known as Yuda rather than Idel, and he was twenty-two years old. Given his passion for writing later in life, it seems likely that he was fully literate by this time, and with a voracious appetite – but not for Hebrew books of religion; instead, he wanted to read Yiddish, and in 1904 the most common Yiddish publications available to him would have been newspapers reporting on the ways that the world – and in particular the mighty Russian Empire - was starting to change.

Despite the fact that modernisation and industrialisation was changing the economy and society that he ruled at a faster pace than ever before, Tsar Nicholas II was a reactionary who resisted reform and liberalisation. A series of defeats in a war with Japan prompted waves of strikes across the more industrialised western cities of the Empire. In late January 1905, such strikes brought Nicholas's capital city of St. Petersburg to a halt. The striking workers marched to the Winter Palace to petition the Tsar – whom they still revered as their 'little father' – asking for better conditions and an elected legislature. The march resulted in a massacre which quickly became known as 'Bloody Sunday', the event widely considered to be the start of the (ultimately) unsuccessful but highly significant 1905 Revolution.

In Rawa Mazowiecka, Yuda was halfway between two large cities which were themselves boiling over with revolutionary fervour. 50km to the west of him was the industrial city of Łódź with a large working class and a combination of proletariat anger and Polish nationalist zeal. Strikes were accompanied with banners proclaiming *"Down with the autocracy! Down with the war!"* 70km to the north-east, Warsaw was even more dangerous; a general strike had been followed by a declaration by the Russian government that Warsaw should be considered a city under siege. From January 30th 1905, Rawa was under a state of emergency, in the heart of the most actively revolutionary part of Poland. Yuda worked for himself as a tailor and would not have been able to go on strike, although he could have easily joined the marches and assemblies that became increasingly common across Poland as the potential flashpoint of May 1st – the international workers' holiday – approached. There were marches, arrests, and some fatalities. Things got worse in Łódź, where June 1905 saw a full-scale uprising which needed six infantry regiments, plus some cavalry, to suppress it. Over half of the officially reported deaths from the fighting were Jews.

The second half of 1905 saw things calming down. The war with Japan ended in defeat, and Tsar Nicholas signed the October Manifesto which promised a series of reforms including universal (male) suffrage and an elected parliament or *Duma*. Two days later a huge demonstration in Warsaw, emboldened by the gains of the

Manifesto, demanded the release of political prisoners. The Cossacks attacked the demonstrators and there was blood on the streets again, but on November 3rd a general amnesty from the Tsar led to the release of over a thousand prisoners in Warsaw, and many more elsewhere in Poland. If Yuda had been arrested, this would have been the reprieve that his daughter Celia told me about 84 years later. Candles were reportedly lit in the windows of Christian and Jewish homes alike as an expression of gratitude and celebration.

November 1905 would therefore have been the time when Yuda would have been making plans for a hurried exit from the Russian Empire to avoid further trouble. The brief notes that I made back in 1989 say that Yuda came to London *"after a tour of Europe – Romania, Bulgaria, Germany France, UK."* Sadly, I've not uncovered any evidence as to whether this is true or false. What is on record is that Yuda arrived in the UK in May 1906, so this would at least be consistent with him leaving Rawa in November 1905 and not appearing in London until six months later. On the other hand, the idea of a young tailor who only spoke Yiddish having the resources, paperwork and connections to travel across multiple countries in 1905-6 without knowing anything more about it does seem a little far-fetched.

There's more which makes me think that London would have been the obvious destination for Yuda to go to straight away from Rawa. He knew people in London. The younger brother of both his mother and his stepmother had been living in London for at least eleven years when Yuda arrived. Lazar Weinberg was born in Skierniewice, just 20km north of Rawa; in fact all the Weinbergs, including Yuda's mother Gitel, were born there. Assuming the Anglicised first name of Louis, he married Rachel Weinbaum in May 1895 in the Great Synagogue in Duke's Place. By 1906 he had a ten-year-old daughter and was living in East London. That wasn't the only connection that Yuda had in London; another family with connections to both Rawa and Skierniewice were living in the West End of London in 1906. The Kriegers moved to London from Skierniewice in the early 1890s with their two young daughters, and set up home in Great Pulteney Street in Soho. Today, Great Pulteney Street is in the heart of the upmarket creative, design and media quarter of the West End; but a century ago it had a significant Jewish community of tailors, dressmakers, cloth merchants and haberdashers centred around Berwick Street Market and the West End Synagogue.

The element that tipped the scales for Yuda in favour of the West End rather than the East End was probably the Krieger's second daughter Dinah. In May 1906 she was seventeen, and already planning for a career on the stage. With the help of these family friends, Yuda started his life in England. He set up in business as a tailor, set to learning English, and began thinking about how he could make his name less of a problem as he navigated his way through life in his adopted country.

The next two documents in which he appears show that the way he named himself was changing. Yuda and Dinah married in August 1908, but the name on the marriage certificate was 'Joe Pshibish'. He signed his name himself, unlike his uncle Lazar who had simply made his mark on his marriage certificate thirteen years earlier. Then in April 1911, he filled in the census form for his household. The address was 7 Thayer Street, Manchester Square – no longer the rather down-at-heel neighbourhood of Soho, but Marylebone; Joe, as he now called himself, was going up in the world as a self-employed ladies' tailor in a much more fashionable part of London. And for the first time on any official document relating to our family, the surname 'Beach' appears in Joe's neat and precise handwriting. He filled in all the columns meticulously; not only the years for which he and Dinah had been married, but the months too. Perhaps most telling is how he chose to complete the 'Nationality' field; where one might expect to see 'Russian subject', or even 'Polish', Joe chose a different answer. Where the question was nationality, his answers for himself and Dinah were simply 'Jew' and 'Jewess'.

Such answers would certainly be consistent with the viewpoint of a supporter of the Bund (*Der Algemeyner Yidisher Arbeter Bund in Lite, Poyln, un Rusland*) – the umbrella movement of Jewish revolutionaries across the Russian Empire. They saw Yiddish as the language not just of a religious minority but of a distinct ethnic group of the proletariat who needed to fight for self-government and cultural autonomy alongside Poles, Lithuanians and Ukrainians. Having said that, Joe's 1911 census return shows that for a member of the revolutionary proletariat, he wasn't doing too bad for himself; he was his own boss, and his home in upmarket Marylebone had five rooms for just the two of them (the two of them became three in January 1913 when their only child was born – a daughter, named Cecelia for Joe's grandfather Kisiel and known to me as Auntie Celia).

Just a few years later, the First World War broke out and Britain found itself on the same side as the Tsar. Was Joe, like Lenin and Stalin at the time, hoping for German success to bring about the downfall of the Russian Empire? If so, there's no evidence for it. The key evidence that does survive from the Great War is a black and white photograph now in the collection of the Jewish Museum in London. Two men are standing outside a tailor's shop, and in the window is a poster topped with a large Union flag. Underneath it proudly states: "*BRITAIN has been all she could be to Jews. JEWS will be all they can be to Britain. Enlist at once in any regiment.*" The man on the right is Joe, and the tailor's shop is his; the other man – with a measuring tape over his shoulders – is Joe's younger half-brother Lipman. Joe was certainly behind the Allied war effort. What I also find interesting in that photograph is the other sign in the window – "*machinist wanted*". Joe the revolutionary was not averse to being an employer himself.

Not only did Joe's shop support the same side that the Tsar was on, but the family (Joe had helped them to come over to London before war broke out) may have had some involvement in standing against the Bolshevik revolutionaries. In March 1917, Nicholas II abdicated and a Provisional Government, still allied to Britain, took power. Jews in Britain of fighting age who were still Russian subjects had so far not been called on to fight on the same side as the Tsar; the allies were too worried that their sympathies would be too strong against the Empire they had fled. But for a few months in 1917, there was a Russia on Britain's side that Jews should want to fight for; so they were given a choice – enlist in the British Army, or join the army of the Russian Provisional Government and go back east. Joe's half-brother Lipman (according to family legend) chose the latter and is rumoured to have ended up as one of the 3,500 'Coventionalists' who were shipped to Russia only to find themselves in a situation where another revolution had overthrown the Provisional Government, abandoned war with Germany and created a Communist state which was an enemy of Britain. Lipman made it back home eventually, claiming to have been saved at the last minute from a firing squad. It also now seems likely that if Lipman was a Conventionalist, it was hardly for any strong anti-Bolshevik feeling; it's more likely that he was back in Poland to bring his wife over to England from the chaos of Eastern Europe at the close of the First World War.

Another important event in Joe's life which happened during the Great War was the founding of the Ben Uri Art Society in 1915. It was Joe himself (under the name of Judah Beach) who wrote a short history of the Society in the 1930s, and of course out of humility and politeness he said little of his role in its early years. The driving force behind the Society's creation was Lazar Berson, an artist who had studied in St. Petersburg and Paris before coming to Britain. In London, Berson found a group of like-minded artists and art enthusiasts who saw the need for a uniquely Jewish artistic and cultural centre, where they could celebrate designs and literature unique to their own cultural heritage. By 1916 the Society had over 100 members and was arranging meetings, recitals and fundraising events – but not yet any exhibitions. Of course, not everyone was a fan; Joe wrote later that a number of Jews in London would say that *"s'iz faran vikhitkere zakhen tsu tun, vi tsu shpieln zikh mit getshkes"* ("there are more important things to be doing than playing with trinkets"). Berson himself shocked the rest of the Society by leaving suddenly for America in the autumn of 1916. Joe was instrumental in keeping the Society going despite Berson's departure, raising funds and purchasing works of art in the hope of creating the permanent gallery which was the main goal of the Ben Uri. That goal was achieved, at least in part, on 17th May 1925 when the Ben Uri Gallery and Club was officially opened at 68 Great Russell Street – across the road from the British Museum. It must have made Joe smile that an uncompromisingly Jewish art collection was taking its place directly opposite the monuments of the Egyptian, Assyrian, Greek and Roman Empires along with all the other imperial powers that had oppressed the Jewish people over the centuries.

As for the location of the Society's growing art collection prior to 1925, Joe's obituary in the Jewish Chronicle gives us the answer. Written in 1964, it tells us that *"his home in Hampstead became a meeting-place for artists, writers, musicians and actors. The first exhibitions of the Ben Uri Art Society were held there, and for many years it housed the permanent collection of the Society."* His home in Hampstead, which he occupied from August 1918 until his death in 1964, was a four-floor townhouse in Holmdale Road NW6 – not bad for a political refugee less than fifteen years after his arrival in the UK. The rest of the Przybysz/Beach family were still living in Soho at the time. They moved out to Cricklewood over the next decade; not far away from Joe, but not quite as desirable an area.

As well as the Ben Uri Art Society, Joe was also very involved in another community group; the Skierniewice and Rawa Relief Organisation, which supported *landsleit* (compatriots) from the two towns from where both Joe's and Dinah's families had come. Even before the Second World War and the Nazi occupation almost completely wiped out the Jewish population of these towns, the Relief Organisation was raising money to improve their quality of life and assist them when asked. The Ben Uri Society played host to an increasing number of refugees from Germany in the years leading up to 1939, and subsequently from German-occupied countries as Jewish artists, writers and thinkers fled from the Nazis. Joe was probably more aware than most of what was happening to the Jewish population of Europe during the Holocaust, and the Skierniewice and Rawa Relief Organisation focused their post-war efforts around finding what few survivors there were from the two towns, and helping them to go to Israel or other parts of the world.

Once the Second World War was over, Joe decided to seek British citizenship. He was Naturalized in 1948 (I'm told that he used to deliberately mispronounce the process, going on to claim that he was just one more thing that was 'nationalised' under the post-war Labour government), and when I spoke with his daughter Celia she showed me the original Certificate of Naturalization which she still possessed. Years later, I became aware that the National Archives held not only copies of these Certificates, but the documentation behind each application; the forms, references and reports from the Metropolitan Police and MI5. This, I was sure, would uncover Joe's revolutionary history, tracked by those who would have been keeping an eye on this busy foreigner with left-wing sympathies.

The files were locked under a 100-year rule, but a simple Freedom of Information request was all it took to grant me access to visit Kew in person and view Joe's file. The Archives were reopening after the initial COVID-19 lockdown, so I was wearing a mask and maintaining careful social distance as I took the (thinner than I was expecting) file from the member of staff at the Archives and carried it to a study desk. Flicking hurriedly through the application forms and postal order receipts, I found the Special Branch report dated 27th February 1948. It was one sentence: *"Metropolitan Police Records contain nothing to the detriment of the applicant or his wife"*. That was it — nothing from MI5, and the notes made on a separate form by Joe's interviewing officer simply say, *"no subversive associations."* The rest of the file adds further details which paint a fuller picture of a respectable, upstanding and decidedly capitalist Londoner. Richard Smith, a zookeeper who lived near Joe, provided a reference which mentions Joe's service as a firewatcher during the Blitz. Joe owned two properties outright by 1948, and his financial situation was certainly comfortable. The state apparatus of the United Kingdom did not see Joe Beach as having ever been any kind of political threat.

Now a British citizen, Joe turned his attention to literature. In the wake of the Holocaust and the genocide of millions of Yiddish speakers, the "Yiddishists" of London and elsewhere redoubled their efforts to preserve and revitalise the *mame-loshen* (mother tongue) which was a central part of Jewish identity for them. He started writing, and became a frequent contributor of short stories to the monthly publication *Loshen un Leben* (Language and Life), produced by a group of Yiddish writers – many of whom were also active in the Ben Uri Society. In 1952 a collection of twenty-one of these stories was published, in Yiddish, under the title *Sheydvegn* (Crossroads); he's still there in the British Library Catalogue, albeit under the name *Yehudah Bietsh*. Shortly after that he became President of the Friends of Yiddish. It was in that capacity that an 80th birthday celebration was held in his honour, including (according to the Jewish Chronicle) *"an almost endless number of tributes paid to Mr. Beach."* Two years later, he passed away peacefully – the last surviving founder member of the Ben Uri Art Society. I'm pleased to say that there were several Beaches present at the Ben Uri's centenary exhibition at Somerset House in 2015, which featured letters and photographs honouring Joe's efforts and achievements.

So far, I have only been able to locate and translate one of Joe's short stories: *Der Anhoyb fin Suf* (The Beginning of the End). It starts in the year 1904 in a Polish *shtetl* simply named 'R', where twenty-year-old Yankel Zilberstein is dreaming of new ideas and far-off places, feeling like he can't breathe in the claustrophobic environment of his little town. He runs away to London leaving everything behind and becomes Jack Silverman, living in Soho with a wife and child. In the First World War he nearly goes back to fight for Russia, but at the last moment he runs away from the train station and stays behind. Jack then becomes successful in business, but when his only son falls for a non-Jewish girl, the resulting drama makes him feel just as trapped and claustrophobic as he did back in Poland – although this time there is no such way out.

If Uncle Joe did start out as a revolutionary taking to the streets in the face of the Tsar's troops, once he got to London it seems that his radical fervour was redirected away from the political and much more towards his artistic and literary passions. If he was a socialist, then perhaps he could be called a champagne socialist; Uncle Joe saw no reason to deny himself the fruits of his business success. He was loyal to his adopted country, while at the same time being intensely proud of the culture and language from which he had come. I wonder whether his move to London was as much triggered by his dreams of new artistic and philosophical horizons (just like Yankel Zilberstein) as it was triggered by the Russian authorities offering an amnesty. Whether Yuda Przybysz or Joe Beach, he *was* passionate about wanting to change the world for the better – but through culture and education, not through turning the world upside down.

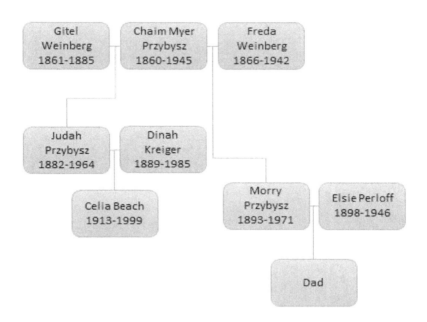

Judah Przybysz. Or Joe Beach. Or Idel Pshibish. Or Yehuda Bietsh (image courtesy of Jewish Museum London)

Judah's birth record, Rawa Mazowiecka, 11 June 1882 (image courtesy of the Polish State Archives in Warsaw, Grodzisk Mazowiecki branch)

Judah (right) with his half-brother Lipman in front of his tailor's shop during the First World War, with a recruitment poster in the window (image courtesy of Jewish Museum London)

MR. J. BEACH'S 80th BIRTHDAY

Jewish Chronicle Reporter

Lovers of Yiddish came in large numbers to Adler House, E.1, on Sunday, to honour Mr. J. Beach, President of the Friends of Yiddish, on his 80th birthday.

There was an almost endless number of tributes paid to Mr. Beach—who was accompanied by his wife—by representatives of many organisations with which he had been associated since he came to London from Poland in 1906.

Among the organisations which sent congratulatory messages were the British Section of the World Jewish Congress and its Cultural Department and the Association of Jewish Journalists and Authors.

Mr. A. N. Stencl, Chairman of the Friends of Yiddish, who presided, said that large gatherings were the answer to those who thought that Yiddish was "going under." In his tribute to Mr. Beach, whom he described as "a man of honesty, uprightness and idealism," he mentioned his close association with "Lashon un Leben" since the first day of its publication.

Mr. S. J. Harendorf, representing the Association of Jewish Journalists and Authors, mentioned the Yiddish stories which Mr. Beach has written.

MR. JUDAH BEACH

Mr. Judah Beach, a vice-president of the Ben Uri Art Society, who died in London on Saturday at the age of 82, was the last surviving member of the small group of art-lovers who founded the Ben Uri in the East End of London nearly fifty years ago, writes Mr. B. Fealdman, secretary of the Ben Uri Society.

Born in Rava, Poland, Mr. Beach came to this country in 1906. He soon made his mark in artistic and literary circles and his home in Hampstead became a meeting-place for artists, writers, musicians and actors. The first exhibitions of the Ben Uri Art Society were held there, and for many years it housed the permanent collection of the Society which Mr. Beach, as its hon. secretary, had helped to build up.

An ardent Yiddishist, he took an active part in the Friends of Yiddish, and for the last ten years had been its president.

JC report on Judah's 80th birthday celebrations, June 1st 1962 (image courtesy of the Jewish Chronicle)

Judah's obituary as published in the JC, 30th Oct 1964 (image courtesy of the Jewish Chronicle)

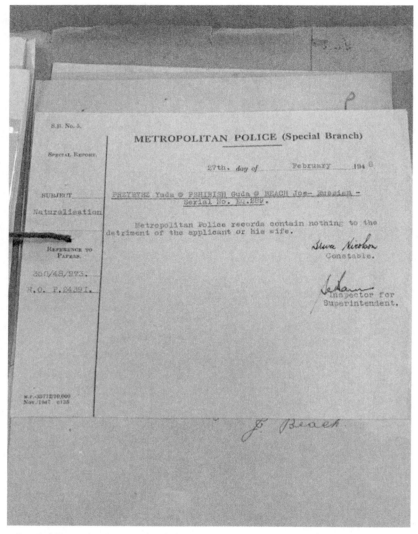

Special Branch report on Judah, 1948 – stating that "Metropolitan Police Records contain nothing to the detriment of the applicant or his wife." (Image courtesy of the National Archives, Kew)

9 Two Russian Bears

There is one side of my ancestry where I can't really say that I was ever told a 'lie', if only because I wasn't really told anything at all about my paternal grandmother's *mishpocha* (family). All I knew was that my dad's mum died when he was very young, and that all his cousins on that side were much older than him for the simple reason that he is the younger son of the youngest daughter. As to the geographical origin of the family, Dad was at least pretty definite that his mum's side were from further east than any other family we had; Russia rather than Poland, and somewhere remote and obscure. I would have my work cut out trying to get anything more than a few names out of any research on the Perloffs.

Talking to family and looking at what some cousins had previously found out, a few details did emerge. My grandma Elsie Perloff was from Bobruisk; a city on the Berezina River, now in Belarus, which was in important fortress town and railway junction in the Russian Empire at the end of the 19th century. The population of Bobruisk in 1897 included 20,000 Jews, making up more than 60% of the city. It was around then that Elsie was born, as her gravestone says that she died in July 1946 aged 48. I knew her parent's names — her father was Bernard, with the Hebrew name *Bentsiyon*; her mother was Esther, who my dad remembers from his own childhood as a tiny, wizened old lady sitting in the kitchen, tutting and *kvetching* over how things were being done wrong by the children and grandchildren around her. Bentsiyon never made it to London, I was told, and he died in Russia. He was Esther's second husband, which was why two of Elsie's sisters (and her one brother) were actually half-siblings. Esther's first husband also died in Russia, so once in London she was the matriarch of her children from both fathers. Her own origin was a complete mystery, with not even her maiden surname known to us. I had visited and photographed her gravestone, which told me that she died in 1944 aged 87. I didn't know when the family arrived in the UK from Bobruisk, although it would have to have been before my grandparents got married in 1927.

That paucity of detail didn't change until a message on an online genealogical forum alerted me to the fact that a new database had been made available on the web. This contained the names and basic details of those admitted to the Jews' Temporary Shelter in Whitechapel in the years leading up to the First World War. I thought it worth a search, and put in all the surnames that I was researching from the various family branches. When I entered 'Perloff', I found a record naming three individuals – Ester, Rochl (Rachel) and Elke (Elsie). This record was from January 1914, and the ages looked like a good fit; Ester was fifty, Rochl was sixteen and Elke was fourteen. The clincher was the other detail that was given; on arrival at the Shelter, they gave their place of origin as Bobruisk. I had found my grandmother.

The Jews' Temporary Shelter was one of a large number of communal charities set up during the period of mass Jewish immigration at the end of the nineteenth century. It's still going, I'm delighted to say, as part of Jewish Care. Simon Cohen, a Polish baker with premises in Whitechapel near the docks, took pity on the immigrants arriving with nowhere to stay, and started opening up part of his bakery to provide overnight accommodation for newly arrived Jews. The political leaders of the community, as they sometimes do, shut it down in 1885 as unauthorised and unsanitary. Simon's ideals were beyond reproach, but some of the *Gantzer Machers* of the Jewish Board of Guardians didn't want an additional source of disease – or of bad publicity. Or even of *good* publicity, as they feared that something like this would only encourage more Eastern European hopefuls to make the crossing to London and add to the burden on the existing community.

Thankfully, there were enough people in the community with the moral foresight to realise that the solution was to establish a safe and sanitary version of Samuel's shelter, and the substance to make it happen. The Poor Jews' Temporary Shelter, for the purpose of helping immigrants in those first few days after disembarking at the Port of London, opened in Leman Street on April 11th 1886. By 1900, the Shelter was being used by thousands of Jewish immigrants each year, and was important enough that passenger ships entering the Thames from Hamburg and Bremen telegraphed ahead to the Shelter to enable staff from the Shelter to be at the docks as the ships arrived. These staff saved huge numbers of new arrivals from being fleeced, mugged or even abducted in their first few hours on British soil. Some of the Shelter's most important work went beyond just providing bed and board for those first few nights; it was involved in helping its residents move on to permanent accommodation and work, or finding passage onwards from London to New York, Canada, South Africa or Australia (the oft-repeated tale told by Anglo-Jewish families that their forebears got off in London thinking that they were in the *Goldene Medina* – the 'Golden Land' of America – is not as likely as people might think. Most likely they knew exactly where they were, but some decided to stay in London even if their original plan was to cross the Atlantic). After the Aliens Act of 1905 made immigration into the UK more difficult, the Shelter helped new arrivals with applications for permanent residence and appeals against deportation, acting as advocates and translating key documents.

Esther and her two daughters couldn't know that the year in which they arrived at the Shelter was the final year of the massive Jewish migration from Eastern Europe that had been going on since 1881; had they delayed their departure from Russia by just a few months, it may have been too late. Almost a century later, I found myself in the Research Room of the London Metropolitan Archives, looking at a rather tattered book embossed on the front: JEWS'

TEMPORARY SHELTER REGISTER OF INMATES. The binding wasn't in great shape, but it held together as I carefully opened it and worked my way through the pages, each one containing about sixteen lines, and each line representing a new arrival into London. Not all the details were filled in for each entry, but a just a glance at each page showed a wealth of names, ages, places of origin, embarkation points, professions and onward destinations that spoke of so many different and amazing stories.

Reaching the page on which my grandmother's arrival was recorded, the other entries on the page were just as fascinating - a mother and three daughters who stayed six days before sailing for South Africa (perhaps to join their husband and father?); a thirteen-year old boot polisher from Odessa, sent to the Shelter by the Reverend Michael Adler, who stayed for twenty-five days and then returned to Russia; and a twenty-year-old painter born in New York who stayed for two days before moving out to live in London. Entry number 516, arriving on 27th January, was 'Ester Perlof', born in Bobruisk and having taken ship from Bremen in northern Germany. 517 and 518 were her daughters Rochl and Elke. They stayed for half a day – perhaps just for a meal and to sit down indoors for a few cold January hours – before moving on, the same day, to somewhere else in London. The only entry on the entire page under 'General Remarks' relates to Ester, and says '140 Rs'. So Esther had some cash on her – 140 Rubles, which in 1914 was equivalent to about fifteen pounds. Enough to make a start on building a life in London for her and her daughters.

Not only did Ester have a modest but important bankroll, but she also knew that she wasn't facing life in a country where she didn't know anyone. All three of her children from her first marriage were already in Britain. Her daughters Manya and Polly had already given their mother British-born grandchildren, although the civil records of their marriages to the respective fathers don't appear until during the First World War. Her son Charles was living in Glasgow, already married and shortly to emigrate from Scotland to New York. It's likely that the location of Rachel and Elsie's half-sisters was the reason why the Perloffs didn't stay in the East End close to the Shelter, but instead moved west to the area around Ladbroke Grove and Portobello Road Market. It was in West London synagogues that the older of the Perloff sisters married a Viennese furrier in 1920, and the younger sister – my grandma Elsie – married Polish tailor Morry Beach in 1927.

By the time of her death in 1944, all four of her daughters from both her marriages were settled in the UK, and she had seen grandchildren and great-grandchildren born in the safety and relative prosperity of a Britain which was a long way from Bobriusk. Her gravestone gave me the only clue I had to her own ancestry – her father's Hebrew name of *Berel*. I couldn't even be sure that this was accurate; would Esther herself have remembered her father's Hebrew name and told someone else in the family before she passed away, or was the name on her gravestone a 'best guess' by her daughters? Without any idea of her maiden name, this seemed like a dead end.

The breakthrough that allowed me to confirm the mystery of Esther's parentage came from an unlikely source. Her son Charles, who moved to New York at the age of 28, lived out his life in the USA but did some travelling in his later years. A genealogy website algorithm suggested to me that I might wish to look at an immigration card issued to a Charles Heckman in October 1963 in Rio de Janiero. I wasn't expecting a 1963 document from Brazil relating to my Great (half) Uncle Charles to unlock a branch of my ancestors from a town in Belarus, but family history research isn't always straightforward. Thanks to the Brazilian authorities asking for Charles's *nome do Pai e da Mãe*, he named his mother as 'Mrs. Esther Plotkin'. She never was Mrs. Esther Plotkin, as her two married names were Heckman and Perloff; her son must have given her maiden surname. Which meant that I could see if, among the limited records from Belarus that did survive, I could find any trace of my great-grandmother Esther's origins.

One of the most frustrating things that can happen in genealogical research is when a major milestone or event falls just outside the point where surviving records can be found – such as the family moving into a country just after a census is taken, or a marriage taking place in that one year for which records have been lost. Thankfully, in searching for Esther Plotkin luck was on my side; she appears just once, aged one quarter. Had she been born just a few months later, no records of her would exist.

'Revision Lists' (*Ревизская Сказка* or *Reviska Skazka* in Russian) were a sequence of ten censuses taken throughout the Russian Empire between 1720 and 1858, only recording those families which were subject to taxation and potential military service. Many Jews tried to avoid being listed, partly for tax avoidance but mainly to save their sons from military service. It has been estimated that in the cities of the Minsk *guberniya* (province) which included Bobruisk, the Jewish population in 1858 was actually 27,000 while the Revision of that year only registered 11,749 Jews. Fortunately (although they may not have thought so at the time), the Plotkins of Bobruisk were found by the official assessor making the rounds of the town on 15th July 1858.

Esther appears as part of an extended family where the head of the household was listed as her grandfather Abram Plotkin, the son of Movsha (the Russified version of Moses). Abram wasn't actually there in 1858, and the list simply says that he left in 1856 with his current whereabouts unknown (Revision Lists, as the name suggests, were revised versions of previous lists – most of the family had been previously recorded in the Revision eight years earlier). Abram's wife Ginda was still there, and five of their children are listed: Zalman the eldest had died three years earlier, the other sons Nison and Berka were listed with their wives and young families, while daughters Khana and Khiena were teenagers as yet unmarried. Nison and Berka had just one daughter each, both with the same name – Estra (Esther) Plotkin – which must have caused at least some confusion in the household. Nison's Esther was six years old, while Berka's was just three months.

Esther's gravestone in London names her father in Hebrew as *Berel*; could this be the same name as the Berka Plotkin in the 1858 list? It was certainly looking hopeful that Berka's daughter was the same Esther who died in Britain in 1944 – her gravestone suggested a birth year of 1857 which was an almost perfect fit. To avoid a detailed digression into comparative diminutive suffixes across Yiddish and Russian, the endings *-el* in Yiddish and *-ka* in Russian both have the same function as an expression of affection or familiarity, like *-y* in English does in the names Harry, Nicky, Richy and so on. So Berel and Berka are the same name, both familiar versions of the Yiddish name *Behr*, which translates to English to mean the animal for which it is also a synonym. In Esther's father, I had found a Russian bear.

The city in which the Plotniks were living was dominated by the fortress which occupied nearly 120 hectares in the centre of Bobruisk. Over 5,000 soldiers were stationed there across the barracks, arms depots, food warehouses, church, hospital and military jail which made up the complex. The fortress provided employment and economic opportunities to the Jewish community of the city, and while the Revision Lists do not give occupations it's certainly possible that Berel/Berka was involved in a trade which serviced the fortress in some way. The family had enough substance to be taxed, and to be listed as 'petty bourgeois' rather than peasants or workers. The part of the city just outside the fortress walls, called the 'polygon', was left clear for strategic reasons with no buildings allowed there – providing an open space for children to run and play on Sabbaths and Festivals.

Life in Bobruisk in the 1850s was relatively good compared to other parts of the Russian Empire, although over the subsequent decades things changed for the worse. Now deep inside the Russian Empire rather than close to the border, the fortress was reduced in importance and a number of fires damaged the city. The railways brought industrialisation and a massive surge in the population of Bobruisk from the 1870s onwards, creating overcrowding and poor living conditions. The rise in antisemitism from 1881 onwards across the Russian Empire was felt in Bobruisk through a series of sporadic attacks and riots every few years. In April 1902, the Great Fire destroyed large parts of the city centre including fifteen synagogues containing nearly 100 Torah scrolls. More than ten thousand Bobruiskers were made homeless. The result was a rebuilding of the city in stone rather than wood, and a rise in revolutionary activity as urban workers realised that they were the only ones who would improve their conditions and freedoms. May Day 1904 saw a General Strike in the city, and the following year the 1905 Revolution resulted in large parts of Bobruisk being temporarily under the control of the *Bund* (the Jewish union of workers across the Russian Empire).

The 1905 Revolution was ultimately put down by the Tsarist authorities, but not before it extracted the promise of some kind of parliamentary democracy from the Tsar. What survives from Bobruisk in 1907 are the electoral registers of those qualified to vote for the Duma (parliament). And in those registers is one Berka Plotkin, son of Abram – still living in Bobruisk aged seventy-four, having survived pogroms, fires, revolutions and more. By this time his daughter Esther was several years into her second marriage, and only seven years away from arriving in London to spend half a day at the Jews' Temporary Shelter. This Russian bear survived well into the twentieth century.

Following the River Berezina upstream for about forty kilometres north from Bobruisk brings you to the small village of Svisloch, where the Svislach river empties into the larger Berezina. In 1897, when the population of Bobruisk was recorded as more than thirty-four thousand, Svisloch was home to 1,787 souls – of whom only 67 were not Jewish. Svisloch was definitely a *shtetl* in the late nineteenth century with a typical mix of farmers, craftsmen, teachers, merchants and tailors. It was here that I found the Perloffs, in the Revision Lists of 1858 and a further edit in 1874. Esther's future husband Bentsiyon appears in the 1874 list as *Bentsiyon Itskovitch Perlov*, aged nineteen – which would make him three years old in 1858, although he doesn't appear at all in the list from that year (it seems that he was named for his own maternal grandfather, which is a pleasing coincidence; my dad's Hebrew name is Bentsiyon after his maternal grandfather).

The Perlovs appear in the Revision lists as an extended family headed by Bentsiyon's father, my great-great-grandfather Itska Evelovich (Isaac son of Joel) Perlov, aged 45 in 1874. Bentsiyon has three brothers and four sisters, from Yakhna the eldest down to little Pesya who is only a year old. What came as rather more of a surprise for me was seeing that he already has a wife and a young child – none of the family had ever given me the slightest hint that Bentsiyon had been married before. Presumably his first marriage ended before the mid-1890s when he started having a family with Esther; I had no idea that both my grandmother's parents were on their second marriage when she was born. Whether Bentsiyon's first wife died, or left him, or was left by him (possibly more likely, based on the possibility of Bentsiyon running away from a small *shtetl* to the big city of Bobruisk, plus the fact that family legend tells me he wasn't the most reliable of husbands), I have no idea. While I am certain that this Perlov family in Svisloch is my *mishpocha*, these Revision List records are almost the only evidence I have of their existence.

There is, however, one further snippet of evidence. Another source which has survived comes from the pages of the *Minskiye gubernskiye vedomosti* – the official newspaper for the Minsk province of the Russian Empire, published from 1838 onwards. It probably wasn't a thrilling read even when contemporary, but it did contain call-up notices when the time came for young men in the villages and towns of the province to be conscripted into the army. Thanks to the efforts of genealogists, many of these notices have been transcribed and made searchable. This is how I was able to find out that in the issue of 28th August 1876, the call-up list included nine young Jews from Svisloch – including Berka Itzkovitch Perlov. In the Revision List of 1874, Berka appears as one of Bentsiyon's younger brothers; perhaps Bentsiyon married young to avoid conscription, which put Berka in the (literal?) firing line as the next oldest son. This second 'bear' was Esther's brother-in-law rather than her father, but it looked like he also had a story to uncover.

Sadly, it wasn't to be a long story. There's no conclusive evidence that he definitely answered the Tsar's call and joined the army, but an additional note in the Revision Lists made a few years later makes it seem very likely. This note tells us that Berka died on 10th October 1878, just over two years after he was conscripted. He is the only member of the family whose death is recorded at all, which could be because he died in uniform. Was Russia at war at the time of his death in 1878? If Berka did serve in the front line at all, it would have been in the Russo-Turkish War of 1877-1878. Not a conflict that many people know of, but a very big deal to the countries of the Balkans and the Caucasus, where most of the fighting happened. It was a particularly nasty and bitter affair, with multiple accusations of atrocities by both sides. This was a war of primarily Christian nationalities against the Ottoman (Turkish) Empire, but of course Jews served in the armies of both sides, as well as getting caught in the middle and forced to flee or suffer attacks. What Berka Perlov thought of fighting on the Christian side against the Muslim Turks we cannot know, although many Jewish soldiers did develop a sense of patriotism and a dual Russian-Jewish identity, finding that their regiments were (in some cases) willing to let them practise at least a certain level of Judaism while in uniform.

Figures for the deaths in the Russian Army from that time make grim reading; of around 260,000 soldiers involved in the conflict, it is estimated that up to one-tenth of that number died in battle, with a further 56,000 wounded – of whom 1,700 died from their wounds. But the biggest killer (perhaps not surprisingly) was disease, which claimed the lives of over 80,000 Russian soldiers during the war. Given that Berka's death at the age of twenty-two is dated a few months after the official end of hostilities, he may have met his end in one of a number of ways; succumbing to a lingering infection, or as part of the Russian force occupying Bulgaria, or perhaps at the hands of the irregular soldiers whose name I never forgot since learning about them in 'O' level History – the fearsome *bashi-bazouks*, who continued to terrorise the Russian forces and their civilian allies well into the twentieth century.

My paternal grandmother's *mishpocha* are still the family about whom I know least, but the few crumbs of evidence which they did leave behind point to a wealth of possibilities and theories over what might have really happened to them. In particular, two characters with the same name have emerged, neither of which I even knew existed before I started researching; two Russian *Behr*s. One, an urbanite named Berka Plotkin, was born in 1833 and grew up to see the city he lived in change beyond recognition to become an industrial powerhouse of factories, railways, overcrowding and revolution well into the twentieth century. The other was Berka Perlov, born twenty-three years later in a small sleepy village by the river; dead at twenty-two, very probably far from home as a soldier fighting for the Tsar in a war that he may not have even understood.

Linking them together is the individual at the centre of this chapter – Esther, born in Bobruisk just a couple of years after the Crimean War and living to see the dawn of the Atomic Age. It was her who, after seeing off two husbands, took her daughters to London with the equivalent of only fifteen pounds in her possession. To take a couple of tiny liberties with the geography of North-West London, she exchanged Belarus for Belsize Park, and Svisloch for Swiss Cottage. And I'm very grateful indeed that she did.

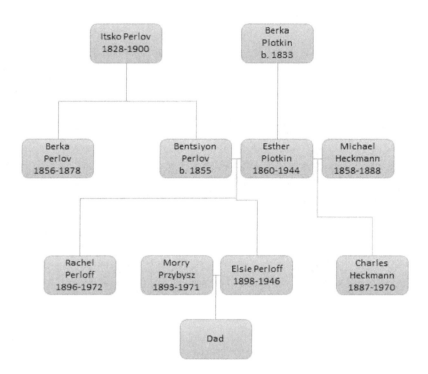

My grandma: Elsie Perloff (1898-1946)

Dining Room of the Jews' Temporary Shelter (image courtesy of Jewish Museum London)

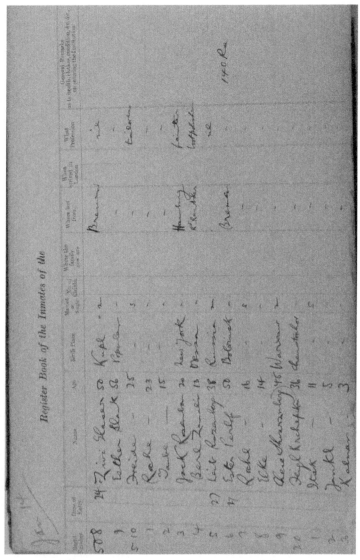

Register Book of the Inmates of the Jews' Temporary Shelter, January 1914, recording the arrival of Esther, Rachel and Elsie Perloff from Bobruisk via Bremen. Source: Records of the Jews' Temporary Shelter held at the London Metropolitan Archives.

10 Yesterday Won't Tell You Anything About Tomorrow

My parents named me Richard, not Reuben. My contemporaries in Anglo-Jewry, born as the 1960s became the 1970s, bear the given names which were popular in the community at the time – Darren, Matthew, Andrew, Michael and Jeremy for the boys; Karen, Laura, Amanda, Nicola and Emma for the girls. Mainstream, non-ethnic, unassuming names that cause no controversy or beg no questions in wider British society. Our parents' generation were broadly similar; the names were slightly different, but the thinking behind them was much the same. Mostly second or third generation immigrants, the names given to Jewish children in 1930s and 1940s Britain included Brian, Stephen, Stanley, Rita, Valerie, Sandra, Carol and Laurence. Nothing 'too Jewish'. But if the parents choosing such names thought that they were doing anything new, they were mistaken. Even in the early 1800s, names which were 'too Jewish' were replaced – Simcha became Charlotte, Leib became Lewis, and Fraenkel became Franklin. Whether in the East End or the suburbs, the idea was the same; look forwards, not back.

After the genocidal horror of the Shoah (Holocaust) and the establishment of the State of Israel, this tendency to focus on the future and try not to talk about the past became even stronger. As I was growing up, that recent past was too raw and too upsetting to be mentioned any more than was necessary. In the same school year as I wrote my biography of my Poppa Sidney, we were told (at the Jewish Day School I attended) about the Shoah, in a lesson I can still vividly remember to this day. Many of my friends had grandparents, uncles and aunts who were themselves survivors, but it wasn't something to shout about. Holocaust remembrance events were quiet affairs. By the time my own children went through Jewish schools, there was perhaps a more urgent awareness that the living witnesses of the Shoah would not always be around; Holocaust education became much more high-profile, and visiting the extermination camps and ghettoes in Poland has become almost a rite of passage for Jewish sixth-formers. Thankfully, wider society in the UK, the US and Europe has been aligned with Jewish communities in ensuring that museums, events, exhibitions and memorials are around to educate and inform future generations about what happened.

My family story is a very fortunate one. All the branches of my ancestry had migrated to London (and onwards in some cases to English-speaking countries outside Europe) by 1914, to the extent that we were not even aware of any close relatives left behind when the Nazi occupation spread across almost every country in mainland Europe. I completely understand that for so many Jewish families, the place names of Germany, Poland, Lithuania and Belarus can only ever mean one thing; countless family members lost to the calamity of 1933-1945. I was taught that what Jews did in mainland Europe was suffer and die. And even in a family relatively unscathed by the Holocaust, that was the image of Europe – particularly Eastern Europe – with which I grew up. There was perhaps one exception to this, which was of course whenever we sat down to watch *Fiddler On The Roof*, but the Jewish European experience was pretty much presented to me as Anatevka, then Auschwitz.

But before Jews died in Eastern Europe, we lived there; and in many cases, we even thrived there. It wasn't all pogroms, blood libels and *If I Were A Rich Man*. The poor, unchanging, inward-looking shtetl did exist, but it wasn't the only Jewish experience, and perhaps not even the majority Jewish experience in Europe. In uncovering the stories of my own ancestry, I've met characters who were fully involved in wider society and taking an active part in the history through which they were living. Koppel Fraenkel was in Vienna doing deals with Moldavian princes; Moishe Przybysz was chatting with priests as he registered his family milestones, and serving repossession notices as well as drinks to the village locals where he worked. Even within the Jewish communities, things weren't always the way that popular imagination would have them. Ester Altmann and her daughter Reizel Kohn were young widows running businesses, while the young men of their town dreamed not of New York or Jerusalem, but Petticoat Lane and Spitalfields.

Then there was the image of Jewish history in the UK which was 'sold' to me and the rest of my generation. We were expelled in 1290, readmitted in the 1650s and then we came to England in two waves; educated *Sephardim* (Spanish & Portuguese Jews) first, and then the poorer *Ashkenazim* (Central & Eastern European Jews) who fled the pogroms as penniless refugees and lived in the East End of London, lifting themselves out of poverty through sheer hard work and entrepreneurial savvy in the teeth of racism and bigotry. The 'gold standard' of immigrant communities, always loyal to the UK even if the establishment wouldn't let us in to their golf clubs and private schools. The trajectory of the community's history has been one of continual upwards movement – the children of cab drivers and tailors becoming doctors, lawyers and politicians. Even the undeniable rise of antisemitism in the early twenty-first century has not seen British Jews as an immigrant group too new and too alien to have a place in the UK, but – in a perversely ironic inversion – as the Establishment. Or part of the Establishment. Or, in the worst cases of contemporary antisemitism, the 'secret power' *behind* the Establishment, pulling strings to make sure they do the bidding of Israel, or the Rothschilds, or the Elders of Zion, or some such nonsense.

Researching those branches of my family which were already in London as far back as the early 1800s has prompted me look beyond the simplistic narrative described above, and think about the parallels between the experience of my ancestors and that of contemporary immigrant groups in the UK. As I write this chapter in early 2022, newspaper front pages are often concerned with migrants crossing the English Channel in barely seaworthy dinghies, so desperate to reach the UK that they pay criminal human traffickers to help them take illegal routes into the country to claim asylum. The current UK government are keen to appear as tough as possible on shutting down such routes and intercepting such boats to force them back to France. Even those who are sympathetic to those seeking asylum are quick to make the distinction between 'genuine' refugees in fear for their lives, and economic migrants who wish to enter the UK for a better life rather than to escape an imminent threat. Another argument often heard is that these Channel migrants must have already passed through 'safe countries' before embarking for the UK, so they should be returned to France or other European nations on their route. Social media often paints recently arrived migrant groups as criminal, keeping to their own cultural and societal standards rather than embracing those of their host country. Even mainstream newspapers occasionally talk of 'no-go areas', where non-British religious courts hold sway and those who are not members of the migrant group dominating the area feel unwelcome and unsafe.

Many – perhaps most – of my ancestors who entered the UK from abroad did *not* do so in immediate fear of their lives. They did so for a better life for themselves and their children. They were, by today's standards, economic migrants. Even the Marcowicz family who left the Russian Empire after 1881 were not expelled by a pogrom, but took a deliberate decision to seek new opportunities in London. The Przybysz and Perloff families in the early 1900s would have passed through (at the time) safe countries before taking ship for London. The Zolty family were already in such a safe country in 1885 when they decided to migrate to London. One could make the case that the UK was hardly 'safer' than some other European countries for Jews around that time, with anti-immigrant groups like the British Brothers' League (whose slogan – *England for the English* – has all the charm and subtlety of its present-day successor groups of thugs and racists) holding marches and rallies with support from prominent politicians. The Kindertransport, which undeniably took in those who would otherwise have died without the UK offering sanctuary, only came much later.

My family history, I have to admit, does provide a number of examples to show that Jewish immigrants were no less likely to take part in criminal activities than any other migrant group before or since. I had no idea before my research started of the extent of Jewish involvement in sex work in mid-nineteenth century London – one can only imagine what the tabloid newspapers of today would make of immigrants running brothels in the middle of the capital. Much has been written on the extent to which Charles Dickens' Fagin is an antisemitic caricature, but to suggest that no such Jewish characters existed in pre-Victorian London would simply not be true. Perhaps the antisemitism lies not in the (accurate) representation of individuals like Lyon Lyons the fence, but rather in the lack of any representations of individuals like his brother Lewis, the tailor and would-be upstanding citizen swindled by the Establishment and dead before he could see his children grow up.

Like any geographically concentrated immigrant group – whether now or a century and a half ago – the Jewish community in the East End couldn't win when it came to assimilation. They were criticised for educating their children in Jewish-only schools and running charity, welfare and housing organisations within the community, despite the fact that the main Jewish school was devoted to changing Yiddish-speaking *shtetl*-dwellers into young men and women who could contribute to British society. Jewish communal organisations were often seen as insular and self-serving, even when bodies such as the Board of Deputies sometimes did more than the angriest member of the British Brothers' League might have done to discourage immigration from Eastern Europe. Perhaps the religious court of Jewish London – the *Beth Din*, which still rules on religious matters – was seen as a pernicious and alien legal system threatening British law, as Shariah courts are sometimes described today in certain parts of the media. While it would be wrong to claim that the experience of contemporary immigrant groups in the UK is identical to that of the Jewish community a century or more ago, there is a great deal of commonality.

Writing the stories of the family members who came before me – almost all of whom I never got to meet – isn't a purely academic exercise. It concentrates the mind on how one might be remembered by generations to come. Not in the way that celebrities or historically 'important' figures might be remembered, but the rest of us; those whose legacy is likely to be limited to close friends or family. I ask myself how accurate a picture of these real people I have been able to paint from the fragments of vital records, census data, newspaper reports and court documents that have been left behind; did any of them have any sense that one day, a descendant of theirs would be trying to piece together their lives and stories from the relative safety and prosperity of the English Home Counties, using technology that was never available to them? I started my family history journey simply looking for facts – names, dates and places so that I could trace my origins on a map – but what I found were stories and personalities. In some cases, I think I can see (or at least suggest) how these stories made the people whom I knew growing up into the characters that they were. My Nanna, a tough decision-maker and businesswoman in the mould of the women who came before her; and my Poppa, determined to dote on his family in the way that his father and grandfather were too neglectful – or too dead – to do.

Then there are the stories that I didn't get to tell in the preceding chapters, for want of space or simply because they were branches of the family about which I knew nothing at all, so there were no 'lies' that I could have been told about them. For example, I discovered that it's almost certain that I have a three times removed second cousin (his great-grandfather and my great-great-great-great-grandfather were the same person) who was a Hollywood actor – Conway Tearle. No, I had never heard of him either, but he appeared in 93 films (mostly silent movies of the 1910s and 1920s) and was at one point thought to be the highest-paid actor in America. His father was Jules Levy, a musician who moved to the USA and billed himself as "the World's Greatest Cornetist". This was the show business branch of the family, starting with Jules's uncle Barnett Lewis Franks - whose claim to fame is that he was part of the original cast of Wilkie Collins' stage adaptation of *The Woman in White* in 1871. Long before that, in his younger days Barnett grew up in Covent Garden, among the brothels and lodging-houses where Elias and Hannah Marks were periodically getting in trouble with the law. Having traced the Franklin/Fraenkel family back to Fürth and Vienna in Chapter Three, multiple other branches opened up through the wives which the Fraenkels took in each generation, most of whom were from well-respected rabbinical families in Vienna or Prague. I could yet discover links to all manner of illustrious cousins or direct ancestors, perhaps even to the point where I could match my wife's direct descent from the Vilna Gaon.

Of course, the blessing and the curse of genealogical research is that it's never finished; unless there is a specific question to be answered (like the date of Grandpa's birthday), there's never a point at which the family researcher can put down their pen, close their laptop and say that they have finished. Each new clue or answer raises more questions, and all you can do is try to assemble enough evidence to be as sure as possible that the way you're putting together the facts is what actually happened. There's no ultimate authority to tell you whether you've got it right or wrong. Genealogy can feel like solving a jigsaw puzzle, except that (a) you don't have the picture on the box to work from, (b) you don't know where most of the pieces are hiding, and (c) many of the pieces don't even exist anymore (but you don't know which ones). Nevertheless, thanks to this hobby of mine I have connected with friendly cousins around the world, learned a little Polish and Russian, got to grips with the Cyrillic alphabet in both printed and handwritten forms, and discovered a huge amount of the historical context in which my ancestors lived.

In 2022, the detailed returns of the 1921 UK Census provided a new treasure trove of information for family history researchers to look into. At the same time, dedicated groups and individuals continue to unearth, translate, digitise and index records from all over the world so that people like myself can have a chance to uncover names and stories that were thought to be lost. There's an odd symmetry in the way that the available information has changed over time; the memories and family stories become fewer as older relatives pass away, but accessible sources of officially recorded 'facts' are becoming ever more numerous through the use of technology as well as the desire of so many to keep these names alive. I'm sure there are more stories and documents that will shed more light on the characters in this book, and perhaps other characters of whom I do not yet know. It's entirely possible – perhaps even probable – that some of what I have presented in this book as fact turns out to be not quite what actually happened. There is a pleasing irony in the likelihood that my attempt to set right the 'lies my family told me' will itself need to be set right in the future.

The branches of my ancestry meet in London, having emerged in a range of locations across Europe. Sometimes it's easy to see the UK as the family's only home, and our inevitable destination all along. Of course, that could not have been the case; a cousin of my dad's told me only recently that he recalls hearing that Myer and Freda Przybysz very nearly settled in Germany when their son Judah paid for them to leave Poland and come to London just before the First World War; given that my Grandpa Morry would have stayed with Myer and Freda, perhaps that counts as a very lucky escape for me. Any of the family branches who moved to London from Europe after 1880 could just as well have gone to New York, as so many others did. Of course, I'm extremely grateful that they did come to London, as I owe my very existence to that fact. I've never considered living anywhere else other than Britain (in fact I'm pretty suspicious of anywhere that isn't north of the Thames and inside the M25) and I'm certainly proud of being part of the story of this part of the world.

So what can a book about yesterday tell me not only about today, but also about tomorrow? Having written so much about my ancestors, I now find my thoughts turning to the future. I have three children, all of whom carry names from back in the family tree in line with Ashkenazi tradition, and all of whom know that they come from a rich mixture of characters across a range of diverse locations. That diversity in the locations, occupations and lifestyles of those who came before makes us realise that the next generation should be free to explore whatever locations, occupations and lifestyles work for them. Some things have endured across generations, and I would like to think that some of these will continue to endure for a long time to come. But our family story is one of change as well as continuity, and the UK is perhaps just another stop in a series of ongoing journeys. Neither wealth nor poverty have lasted long in the stories that have been uncovered here; maybe that is a lesson about what really survives and what doesn't, or maybe just a reminder of the fickle hand of fate that can influence the course of events just as much as the behaviour of individuals can.

Most families will have their myths – whether created by invention, distorted by simple error or rewritten to cover up some other story which was considered unacceptable. Seeking out the truths and the not-quite-truths in the stories that were handed down in my family has made me aware that these myths are still valuable, even when they have been disproved. The fact that something has been misremembered or deliberately changed is itself important, and can point us to the reasons why the family myth fails to match the facts once they are uncovered. The value in all family stories, because they are ultimately about real people rather than just cold hard facts, can be found in both the truth and the lies.

.

ACKNOWLEDGMENTS

There are many people who deserve to be mentioned here, not just for the months that I have been working on this book, but for the many years of research that got me to a point where it became even a possibility. I really ought to start with my parents – who are not only altogether fantastic humans, but also encouraged me in this *meshugas* right from the start. It was Mum who came with me on those first pre-digital visits to trawl through microfilms of census returns and civil records back when this all needed to be done in person. Plus of course I should really thank them for the wealth of characters and stories in my ancestry, which has made this book such a joy to write. Thanks also to those relatives of mine who are no longer here in an obvious sense, but who gave me their time and their love while they were around – my Nanna and Poppa, and wonderful Auntie Celia.

On a more practical level, there are the people without whom my research would never have got past dead ends – John David Lyons (my Antipodean cousin), Gisela Blume for help with the Fürth community archives, Jonquil Simons and Steve Morris on the Franklin side and Dad's cousin Michael whose knowledge of the Beach family has been a huge help. Then there are the online resources, many run by volunteers, which have allowed me and so many others to discover our families' past. Thanks also to the official organisations holding records, in particular the National Archives in Kew, the London Metropolitan Archives, Rachel Lewis at the Jews' Temporary Shelter, the General Register Office, the British Newspaper Archive, the Jewish Museum London and the Polish State Archives in Grodzisk Mazowiecki. And to Julian Knopf at Gander Photography for the cover design.

Finally, to those closest to me who have provided support, enthusiasm and a healthy dose of book/life balance throughout this process. My brother Darren, Mum & Dad (again), and above all my wife Karen and the next generation now adding their stories to the ones here – our children Josh, Shosh and Sam. You three are part of the future that the characters in this book dreamed of.

ABOUT THE AUTHOR

Richard Beach is an amateur genealogist, a former geography teacher and currently works as a software consultant when he absolutely has to. Despite his parents' pleadings, he never became an accountant. He lives in Hertfordshire with his wife Karen and three children. This is his first book.

Printed in Great Britain
by Amazon

78277112R00092